One Man's Tail
By: Eric James Faulk

This book is dedicated to all the people that influenced me to complete what I have started. Most of all to my father. You have taught me how to be a man and a father through the way you lived your life. You are the best example of what a man is supposed to be. I love you more than you will ever know.

Table of Content

CHAPTER ONE
Another good day at the swap meet

Today started off like any other day in my life. I took a drive out to L.A. from Woodland Hills to visit one of my best friends, Toni. Toni and I had met in college some years ago. I graduated about two years ago, but he chose to stay around to "finish up" as he would say. I always hated the drive to L.A. The traffic was always crazy and the people were always rude, much different from the folk in Mississippi. Cool, laid back, it was home.

I moved to California when I decided to go to USC for a track & field scholarship. I received my Bachelors in Business Management and after that I chose to stay in Cali because of the job opportunities. Plus there was so much more to do out in Cali than back in Mississippi.

The weather was always great out here in Cali. Sunshine, palm trees and the temperature stayed at 75-80 degrees. I pulled up at Toni house about 3:45 in the afternoon. We were supposed to go to Slauson Swap Meet to pick out some clothes and maybe pick up some women at the same time. Man, the times me and Toni had together. I could tell you so many stories about the mess we use to get ourselves into. Toni was never on time. He's one of those "last minute" kinds of people. I'm surprised he never shit on himself as long as he waited to do anything.

As usual, he appears from the house yelling. See, he lived with his mom, and living with your mom isn't the childhood experience you would like it to be when you are a grown ass man with no aspirations in doing much more than hanging out all night, sleeping all day and occasionally going to class. Toni didn't have a job but he side hustled for cash just to get by. But he is a good guy and has a big heart when you finally get to know him. "Aright I hear you, I wish you would shut the fuck up," he mumbles to himself as he gets in the car.

"Sssoooo, how are you doing dawg?" I asked him knowing that he was upset. "I'm straight cuz, just sick of this. I need to move out and get my own spot" he replied. He always said that, but I knew that it was going to take his mom to kick him out for him to leave. I drove off from the crib with his mother in the rear view. She was very young looking to have a son my age, hell I would hit it if she gave me a chance and he wasn't my best friend. I know you're thinking that was a bad statement to say about someone's mom, but hey, that's just me. I love women, can't help it.

My mom always said that I'm just like how my grandpa was. We both just loved the women. That's probably why I have so many uncles and aunts on my mom's side of the family. But I didn't want to go out like that, I want to have my baby or babies with one women. Someone I'm going to be with for the rest of my life, and her name is Candy.

Believe it or not, I met Candy on the internet. I was in some chat room and came across her screen name, "justlikecandi", and decided to see what she was all about. She had great conversation and an outstanding personality. She didn't have a picture, but I didn't care. We talked for a month and then we decided meet up at a nice coffee shop in Hollywood because that was an area that we both lived close to. She stayed in a little apartment in downtown LA over by USC campus with two roommates. Both of them were cute, but they couldn't compare to Candy.

On the day that we met I made it to the coffee shop first. I was kind of nervous because I didn't know how she would react to me. Most of the time ladies are attracted to the gangsta type of cats. I'm far from a gantsta. I'm a tall, light-brown skinned, football linebacker looking guy. I dress in athletic gear unless I have somewhere to be like today. I wore an white dress shirt with no tie, black slacks and church shoes. From how I dress I really don't get much play out here in Cali until I open my mouth and my down south accent comes out.

When she came in I knew it was her because of the black dress with red rose dress that she said she would wear. She was shorter than I imagined but she had the nicest, smoothest caramel skin. I loved that. Her hair fell down to her shoulders and she had a body that most women would kill for. I didn't know, but she had a certain confidence when she walked. She didn't have the "look at my ass" walk that a lot of women have, but the "I'm here" walk.

When she looked in my direction I waved to her. "This is the moment of truth right here," I said to myself. When she walked up it was funny because she hit me up like "I know you". That statement took me by surprise, "you do?" I replied to her. She nodded her head then replied, "You remember a girl named Tasha?" I thought for a minute and then I almost pissed my pants. I met Tasha at a track meet we both were running at when I was in college. Tasha used to run for UCLA. When I met her she was with another female but I didn't pay any attention to her because Tasha had a P.H.A.T booty. I still can't believe it. She was what we call down south a "stallion" or had a "Sprinter" body. Well to make a long story short, Tasha I had sex and that was that. "That was you with Tasha at that track meet?" I asked Candy. "Yes that was me" she replied with a smirk. "What's that look fur?" I asked her. "Let me just say it like this, I know what happened and let's leave it like that. I should leave right now" she told me. I replied to her with confidence "but you're not, because if you was, you would have rolled when you saw me." She turned around and was about to leave until I ran to her. "Come on, I was just joking" said to her. She knew I was a joker from all the conversations we had on the phone and over the net. She just wanted to see how I would react if she did that I later found out.

We talked and got along better than I imagined. Her personality was even better in person. I discovered that day that her and Tasha were both from Georgia and met each other right before I met them. Shortly after that Candy transferred schools due to a "conflict of interest" with her one her teachers. Meaning that he tried to get some from her and couldn't take no for an answer.

We talked and laughed until the coffee shop closed. I had to go to work the next morning, so I didn't invite her over to my place. She told me it was a pleasant change from the "hit it and quit it" guys she had come in contact with lately. "Hey what can I say? It's the country in me" I would always say when someone gave me a compliment like that.

I know you may be thinking, "If he has a good girl in his life, why go out looking for more women?" Well, like I said before, I love women. White, Black, Asian, whatever, as long as she had a banging body I was cool. But now for some reason, I have been mainly attracted to my sisters. When I see fine black women walk by, I just want to make all of them mine. But that's not how the world is, but I do wish I was Moorman sometimes.

Toni and I made it to Slauson in no time. We took the back streets instead of the highway. My car wasn't fancy at all. It was a black two door Sentra with tinted windows. It got me from point A to B, and that's all that mattered to me. When pulled up it was like a black family reunion out there. Nice cars, nice women, "I LOVE L.A." I said to my friend.

We parked the car and proceeded to the entrance. I felt the eyes watching me as we entered the swap meet. I always stood out because I had a different kind of swagger than these Cali cats and the ladies loved it. Not because it was better but different. Most people like a little difference in their lives. Something about the abnormal really attracts people.

It's funny, the swap meet never changed but it was always packed full of people. Cali weather made it possible for women to wear whatever they wanted, whenever they felt like it. They would walk around showing cleavage, short pants that showed most of their booties. But what I liked the most was when women wore the

Capri type pants. The way they showed a woman's natural curves made me crazy.

Toni and I went to the usual clothing spot. This place was casual yet dressy. When I go to the club, I like to be dressy but not too dressy. I'm not one of those cats that go to club to drink and hold up the wall, I like to get my boogie on. Women like to see how you move on the floor so hopefully you move like that in the bedroom. When I was younger I used to be grinding all on the floor. Those were my college days when I was young and full of energy, now I leave all that at home. Don't get me wrong, if the feeling is right I will but not all the time.

I picked out a black and white suit. It was a solid black long sleeve shirt with a white design in a diagonal position and solid black slacks. Toni got an all forest green suit. It was clean, but mine was better.

The two of us walked out of the store to see two good-looking females checking us out. Me personally, I'm a very outspoken person and Toni doesn't like it all the time. But when it works out he enjoys the fruits of my labor. I walk over to the two ladies. "How you pretty ladies doing today?" I asked. "Man shut up. I don't feel like talking to them" Toni mumbled to me. "We're fine, how about yourselves?" the one on the right replied. She had a young look to her but you could tell she was older because of how she dressed. She had on a pink Baby Phat shirt with some dark blue Baby Phat jeans. The jeans fit just right around her hips and ass, but the shoes told it all. She had on some nice heals on that showed she had just gotten a fresh pedicure. Her friend had on a pink Apple Bottom sweat suit and some pink and white Nike boots. Both of them looked damn good. "Chilling, just doing some shopping so we can hit the spot tonight." I answered. "What spot you hitting?" she asked. "Some spot down sunset and then check out some spots my dawg right here told me about." I said. "Dawg? Where are you from?" the one on the left asked. "I'm from the M.I.S". "The M.I.S?" They both asked together.

"Mississippi" I replied. "Oh, a country boy, and what about you?" the one on the left asked Toni. "LA, over on 106th and Western" Toni replied with arrogance in his voice. "My sister's baby daddy stays over there" the one the right said. "Oh how rude of us, my name is Sammy and this is my dawg Toni" I said quickly. "This is Jazmin and I'm Shadow" the one on the right said. "Shadow?" I said in a questioning manner. "Yeah, you don't get my real name, not yet" she said with a wink. "Nice to meet you ladies" I said as I took both their hands and politely kissed each one. "Well we have to go, you ladies have a good day" I told then before me and Toni turned and walked away. We did this all the time. Sometimes the females would holler at us for our number or give us theirs but most time we were assed out. All in all of it was funny to me. But when it worked, I would rather give a female my number because if they was really into me, they would call, if not, I wouldn't hear nothing from them. "Hey! How you going to leave like that!?!" Jazmin called out to us. "Got'em" I said to Toni with a smile. "What's going on lil momma?" I replied. "If you guys want to hang out tonight, here's a number where you can reach us at" Jazmin said reaching a piece of paper out towards Toni. "You know what? When you get free, here's my number, give us a call" I said reaching out one of my business cards from my job. That one always got them. To them in meant that meant I had a good job and money. They took the number and we said our goodbyes then left the swap meet. "Another good day at the swap meet" Toni said as we drove out of the parking lot.

CHAPTER TWO
Why did I do what I just did?

Getting ready to go somewhere has always been a long process for me. I take a long shower; dry off before I get out the shower so I won't get water everywhere. Make my way to the bedroom and make sure I'm totally dry, then put on deodorant. I rubbed my body with cocoa butter so I would have a scent of edibleness on my body. It was funny though, when I get out the shower and go through this process of cleanliness, I always feel a sense of loneliness. Besides the old school slow jams playing in the background, the apartment felt quiet and empty. That's why I usually have someone over. Candy, Toni, anyone except the females I just met. I always met them somewhere else. Can't have a lot of different women knowing where you live, that is not good for business.

While I was sitting on the edge of the bed in deep thought the phone rings, "hello" I said after hitting the speaker button on the phone. "What's up baby?" I heard Candy say. "Nothing much baby girl, just here rubbing lotion on myself feeling sexy" I replied to her. She laughed, "Well maybe I should come over there before you go to the spot?" I hated when she did that. She knows if she comes over and we get intimate I'm not going to want to go to the spot, and then I would have to hear Toni's mouth, "Man cuz, you got me over here ready to go and now you chump out!" So I told her, "Knaw baby, I'll hit you up tomorrow after I get up. We can go have breakfast or something." "Ok baby, but I'm going out with the girls, so not too early" she responded. I hated her friends, they always into something. Not my girl, just leave her alone. But who am I to talk.

About time I got done getting dressed, picked up Toni, and arrived to the strip club it was 9:50. This was good because all the guys that had been in the club since after work didn't have any more money to give away. That means we can flash some cash for the new girls just getting to work and get all the attention we wanted. One thing about me, I have the highest respect for people that can do something I can't. Like a construction workers, military personnel, landlords, but especially strippers or shall I say exotic dancers. I could never get up there and get naked in front of a gang of strangers every night. Not that I have anything to be ashamed of but that's just not me. So they get the up most respect from me.

This spot was an illegal type place. See in California they have laws about drinking in strip clubs. If it's a totally naked strip club, no alcoholic drinks, if the women wore bikini or topless you can only drink beer. It wasn't like that in down south. You can drink whatever you wanted in the strip club son matter what the girls had on. You can touch them and whatever for the right amount of cash. Here they had a metal bar around the stage that you could not pass. Not fun at all. So guys would make back alley type strip clubs to have a freer experience.

When we got there I knew it was shady. It looked like an abandoned old bar. No lights and it were located in a back alley. I didn't like places like that. Cats out in LA are on some jacking shit. But I have faith in my man Toni. Toni and I were sitting in the car, and I said to him "what the hell, dawg?" "Just wait until you get inside" Toni responded. So we walk up to this cast iron type door. Toni knocked three times then a little window in the top middle of the door opened, a pair of eyes veered out, looked around and then the little door shut. I heard a big "clank" sound and then the heavy door opened. A guy stepped out that was so big that he made me look like a midget. "Step in" he said with a deep voice that would make Darth Vader sound like a bitch. We stepped in trying not to show any fear. The door closed behind us. I heard Luke's song "Big Girls" playing in the background. He patted both of down and he told us "have a good time homies". We only paid ten dollars to get in and that reminded me of Mississippi, because the strip clubs here in Cali usually hit you for twenty to get in.

When we walked through the dark blue curtain, it was LIVE! There were cats playing dice on a pool table in the back left corner, the bar they had was located in the center back, it looked like one you would see in your house, and the DJ was spinning records on the right. The stage was located in the middle of the room. It was like two inches off the ground and had round tables surrounding it on all sides. The girl that was dancing was "twerking" it. That is a country word meaning she was dancing her ass off. I wasn't expecting this. I felt like I was at home. I went to the bar and got a Hennessey and Coke and Toni got an Incredible Hulk. He always bought the most expensive drinks because when we went out, it usually was my money we were spending. It was cool, he looked out for me one time that I really needed it so I didn't mind returning the favor.

We took our seats and it was like ten other guys in there watching the show. They looked like they had about twelve dollar bills between all of them. I gave Toni sixty dollars and he went to the DJ stand and got sixty ones. When he came back I took thirty and I gave him thirty. We sat there as the girl made her way over to us. Toni always tried to play cool when we went to the strip club. So I would always set him up. I called her over and whispered in her ear "I got fifteen for you to break off my home boy". She went over to Toni and started grinding on his lap. He sat there with his arms crossed like he was too good to have her dance on him. So she started bouncing that ass on him so hard that the vibration made his hat fall off his head and he was about to fall off the chair so he grabbed onto her like she was a bull and he was a cowboy about to get bucked. It was so funny everyone laughed and he couldn't help but laugh himself. She gave him a kiss on the cheek, collected her money from me and went to a door by the bar with green curtains on it. "Damn dawg, I thought you was going to bite it" I said to him with a big smile on my face. "You know I'm just like a cat, I always land on my feet" he said with a laugh. We always had a good time together.

The waitress came over to see if we wanted a refill. She had on a nice little outfit that shows all of her best features, her breast and ass. I saw Toni's eyes light up when she walked up to our table. He like the young looking girls, me, I always felt like a child molester if she didn't look twenty-two and above. "Would you guys like another drink?" she asked. "Yeah give me a Hen and Coke and an Incredible for my dawg." I said. She nodded and left to get the drinks. Toni leaned over to me and said "I'm going to fuck her tonight". I asked him "yeah right, how you going to do that?" "In the private room, they do that here" he replied. I said "fo' real? Do what you do". She came back and told us "that will be twenty dollars". I gave her the money and then I saw Toni signal for her to come over to him then whispered something in her ear. She nods and walks over to a guy sitting in a chair by the bar. She walked back, grabbed Toni by the hand and they went over to the guy sitting in the chair. Toni gave him some money and they went through the door beside the man.

I was at our table sipping on my drink, still tipping and then the next girl came to the stage. I observed her as she walked to the stage. I started at her feet and worked my way up. She had on a long blue evening dress. It had a glitter design on it and a long split on her right leg that stopped just below the hip area. The dress hugged her body just right around her hips, ass, and her small waist. Her breasts were a nice mouth full size and her face, wait a minute, "OH SHIT, THAT'S TASHA!" I said to myself. I wanted to laugh out loud but I held it in. I sat there with a big smile on my face, waiting until the moment that she noticed who I was. She went to the left side of the stage. The way she moved her body way better than I thought she could. She took her time dancing and singing to herself the song that was playing. Her movements were slow and sleek. I was highly turned on by this. She slowly let the dress slide down her body and then let the dress drop to the floor. She had a dark blue thong on with a dark blue lace bra. She danced slowly towards me and I could have been her mother the way she reacted when she saw me. The look of surprise came over her face, I really didn't know if it was surprise or embarrassment.

She quickly went to the guy at the other table and danced for him but the whole time looking back at me. I pulled forty dollars out of my pocket and held it out for her to come to me. She shyly came over to me and shamefully danced for me. "You don't have to act like that, ain't nothing wrong with you making some money." I said to her so she would calm down. She smiled and said "thanks". She took the money, backed up and started snaking her body just for me. She unlatched her bra, walked to me slowly. She grabbed the back of my head and put my face in between her breast. They were soft and smelled like Curve for women. I can't lie, that shit made my dick hard. I wanted to take one of those juicy brown breasts in my mouth but this right here was already way beyond a red light. "This is my girl's best friend" I thought to myself. So I pulled back and said to her, "go make that money, you can't stay here the other cats are paying too." She nodded and continued her show.

About the time that Toni came back out Tasha was finishing up her turn. He came out saying, "Yep that was well worth the change. A brotha can go home now." "I'm ready when you're ready" I told him. "It's already twelve." Tasha came out from the back fully dressed in an oversized UCLA sweat suit. "You know you shouldn't wear that around here, you don't want to take a chance on messing up you scholarship" I told her. "Yeah, your right, can you give me a ride home?" she asked. "How you get here?" I asked with a high-pitched toned voice. "I caught the bus; do you really want me taking the bus this late at night? Are you that cold?" she asked me. "You better be glad that your girl is my girl" I said to point that fact out so that she wouldn't think of trying anything slick. "Where is my girl while you all in the streets?" she asked. "She went out with some friends, hey why you didn't go?" I asked. "She didn't tell me anything about it. We don't really talk like we used to since y'all got together and I started working here. Between school and hustling this money, I don't have time for anything" she replied. I nodded and then said "oh, this is my man Toni right here". "You're cute Toni, why all the cute ones ride together?" she said taking Toni's hand. Toni licked his lips "Sammy didn't tell me about anything as delicious as you?" he told. "I don't know, maybe he wanted to forget about me" she said before cutting her eye at me. "Well if y'all ready…" I said motioning to the door. I walked out followed by the two.

We jumped in my car and drove off. Everyone was quiet until Tasha spoke. "What y'all got going tonight?" she asked. "We about to head to the tilt." I answered. "What you got going?" Toni asked her. "I'm probably going to sit up for a minute, sip on something, and watch a movie. It's the weekend and I just want to relax. School and work can break you down." she replied. "You go to school? Which one?" Toni asked. "UCLA" she answered pointing to her sweater. "All the fine girls go to UCLA." Toni said with a harsh tone in his voice. We pulled up to her apartment, which she shared with one other girl from the college. "Thanks for the ride. Y'all want to come up for a quick drink?" Tasha offered. "Knaw, its late we better go" I said. "Knaw I will take that drink." Toni said quickly. "Come on, one drink, its free" he said to me. I didn't have a good feeling about this, not a good feeling at all. "Alright, one drink." I replied reluctantly.

When we walked up stairs to the apartment it was totally dark. Tasha opened the door and let us in. "Where's your room mate?" Toni asked. "She went home for an emergency." Tasha said while taking off her shoes. "I have cranberry and vodka, or some hen." "Do you have any coke?" I asked. "No, sorry" she replied before going to the bedroom. Toni and I made us cranberry and vodka drink and we sat on the sofa. I turned on the TV with the remote, "I'm gonna get you sucka" was on. "OH SHIT, THAT'S MY MOVIE!" Toni yelled with a half jump off the couch. "Sit your crazy ass down" I said to him with a laugh. Tasha comes out with nothing but a tee shirt and panties on. Toni and I looked at each other like "what the fuck?" Seeing the looks on our faces she said "I hope I don't make you guys uncomfortable being like this. I can go put something else on." "Knaw, knaw, you cool just the way you are. This is your spot." Toni quickly answered before I had a chance to say anything. She sat on the love seat to the left of the TV and we sat on the long couch directly in front of the TV. My eye kept wondering over to her. She got up and walk in front of us to get a drink. Toni nudged my arm when she was in the kitchen. "We can FUCK!" he said with excitement. "You can, I can't. This is my girl's friend MAN!" I said. "But." Toni stopped because she was on her way back. "What are you to talking about? I know y'all ain't being bad over here are you?" she said in a very seductive way. "What if we are?" Toni asked. "Well it all depends on what you are talking about" she replied. "We were talking about you and how sexy you are." Toni said to her, then sitting up in the couch. "A fine time for Toni to be the aggressor when talking to a female. Must be that act right juice he been drinking all night." I thought to myself. "Really, well what can I say?" she said before standing up and walking towards us. I knew it was time to leave, but something was keeping me from standing up, of yeah, it was my dick. She came over to me and started rubbing my dick with one hand and with the other she put her index finger in Toni's mouth. "What y'all wanna do then?" she asked us. My mind was telling me "get the fuck out" but my body wanted to stay and enjoy the pleasures she had in store for me and my friend. "What is a man to do?" I thought to myself.

Before I knew it Toni had started kissing her and she had my dick in her hand slowly stroking it up and down. Her hand felt nice and smooth against my manhood. I pulled up her shirt so I could get to her breast and started rolling my tongue around the nipple, then firmly placed it in my mouth. I began sucking on it nice and gently. I wanted to do this earlier tonight at the club. Her breast was warm and felt good in my mouth. My mind kept taking me back to when me and her had sex some time ago. In the back of my head, when I saw her tonight, I knew this was going to happen, but not like this. Toni had stood up and took off his shirt. I kissed her neck, she leaned down to kiss me on the lips, but I turned my face away and began sucking her other breast. By then Toni was already naked as a Jay bird. "Damn boy, you fast!" she said to Toni. I laughed to myself. "That's two first in one night for Toni.

Aggressively igniting something with a female, and not going at it at a snail pace." I thought. He turned off the TV. Toni and I was the same, he didn't want to see me and I damn sure didn't want to see him.

This was mess up, this will be my second time having sex with Tasha, my girl's friend, and I haven't slept with Candy yet. She pushed me back on the sofa, got down on her knees in between my thighs and placed my penis inside her mouth. Her mouth was so warm and wet; she really knew what she was doing. Toni grabbed her hips and made her stand up while she was sucking me. He took off her panties and started eating her from behind. I laid on the sofa slouched down with my pants half way down. Toni must have been eating her really good, because she started moaning while my penis was in her mouth. The vibration from her moans added an extra sensation that made the head she was giving me feel like I have never felt before. Toni got on his knees so he could get all the pussy in his mouth and continued doing his thing. "Straight porno stuff" I thought.

Toni was doing his thing back there because she was moaning crazy, which was fine to me, because the more she moaned the better it felt on my dick. She sucked me like I loved, with two hands and a whole lot of spit. Then Toni must have slid his penis up in her pussy because she took my penis out of her mouth and said "OOOHHH". I felt her body start jerking back and forth slowly. "Oh, oh, oh" she moaned then she put my dick back in her mouth then the moans became muffled again. "Mmm, mmm, mmmm" she continued to moan. I could hear the smacking from Toni pounding that ass. "Say Sammy, lets switch" Toni said to me out of breath. "Alright" I replied. She took me out of her mouth and stood up. I stood up and walked to the back of the couch to take off my clothes, while Toni sat on the couch to receive some of the sweetest mouth I had ever felt. I could hear the good slurping from her mouth as she gave Toni head. I got my clothes off and got behind her. She was in the same position as before, legs straight while bending over. Her ass looked like a heart shaped box of candy filled with chocolaty creamed goodness. I took my dick in my hand and slowly slid my dick head into her flowing waters. "DAMN" I heard her say as I guided it in. I pushed it in as far as it could go and then slid out slow until the tip of my penis almost came out of her pussy. Grabbing her by her waist I guided myself deep inside of her one more time before I started pumping faster, then a little faster, then faster until I was in my usual rhythm. "OOHH YEAH! FASTER, FAASTTER YOU FUCKING BASTARD" she screamed. So I sped up a little, but not too much, did want to be cum prematurely. Toni would never let me live that down. I gave her ass a smack on the right cheek; I remembered from last time that she like that. "OOOOHHHH" she said.

"Hey dawg we going to have to do something different." I said to Toni. "Alright" he replied. So I backed away from her and she laid down on the sofa and he said "go ahead cuz" So I got on top of her and slid my dick in. Her legs were spread wide and she used her hands to push my ass so I could go deeper inside of her. She was a freak, for real. I was bracing myself with my arms when Toni got in front of me with his ass in my face. "WHAT THE HELL YOU DOING?" I yelled. "I'm going to get some head from her". He replied. "Oh you need to say something, no body want to see your ass," I told him the whole time still putting the dick on her. "Y'all crazy," Tasha laughed. But the laugh quickly turns back to moans of pleasure. I could feel her pussy grab and release my dick with every stroke until I couldn't take it anymore. "I'm about to cum" I told her. "Me too" she said. So I started stroking in and out faster and faster. "AAAAHHHH, AAAAAHHHHHH" she started to yell. She moved Toni out of the way and wrapped her arms and legs around me tight until I felt the sexual explosion come out of me into her. "AW FUCK, AW FUCK, TAKE THIS SHIT TAKE ALL THIS SHIT!" I yelled as the last bit of my cum was injected into to her warm, tight, wet pussy.

I laid there for a second then I got up and went to the bathroom. I guess Toni put her back in doggie style because all I heard was her

booty smacking and her screaming, "YES, YES, FUCK ME, FUCK THIS SHIT OUT OF THIS PUSSY!" As I washed myself off, the feeling of betrayal swept over my body. I felt dirty and unworthy to have a good woman like Candy in my life. All of a sudden it was quiet. Toni knocked on the door and asked, "say cuz, can I use the bathroom?" I walked out with a towel around me and said nothing. He went in and I heard the shower going. I sat at the kitchen table with the drink I didn't get to finish. Tasha walked over with a robe on. "What's wrong?" she asked. "You know what's wrong, this. This should not have happened. I'm with your home girl, and look at us, up in here fucking like this." I told her. "Yeah, but what happened, never has to leave this apartment. It happened, but now it's over, you love her right?" she asked. "I don't want to talk about that right now; it will only make me feel worse than I already feel right now. I just need to know that what happened here, stays here, right?" I requested. "Boy don't even trip, if I can keep my stripper job under wraps, this ain't nothing, just sex" she reassured me. "Pinky swear?" I said with a smile. We both laughed and grabbed each other's pinkies and shook. Toni came out the bathroom fully dressed, "we going to have to do this again, girl you know you got the bomb".
Sometimes that cat is so out of line. "You ain't dressed yet, cuz?" he asked me. "Knaw, I'm doing that now." So I got dressed, we gave her a hug and rolled out. On the way to Toni's house, he slept. In the silence my mind was racing one hundred miles a minute. "Why did I do what I just did?"

CHAPTER THREE
The day after

I woke up the next morning about 10:30 with the after taste of liqueur in my mouth and a heavy burden on my chest. It was a bright, sunny California Saturday. It was the middle of winter but it felt like a Mississippi Spring day. I got used to my winters being nice and calm since living in Cali. The weather in Mississippi gets quite cold this time of season.

As I brushed my teeth, I tried not to look in the mirror. I couldn't stand to look at myself knowing that I did the most wrong thing that you can do to your significant other. The phone began to ring in the background; I already knew who it was. I walked over and read the caller id. It read "Candy Austin". I didn't know if I wanted to answer the phone. "Did Tasha tell her? Was she calling to break it off with me" I thought to myself. "Fuck it" I said before picking up the phone. "Hello" I said like I had just been woken from my sleep. "Did I wake you up?" Candy asked. "Knaw, just brushing my teeth, what's going on baby?" I replied. "I have a problem to discuss with you!" she said with attitude in her voice. "Oh shit, here we go" I thought before answering. "What I do?" I asked with a concerned voice. "Nigga you know. Wasn't we suppose to get some breakfast this morning?" she asked me. I took a deep breath of relief, and laughed to myself. "Sorry baby, me and Toni had a long night last night, I'm sorry. He didn't want to go home" I told her. "So I take it you and your friend had a good time?" she said. I knew she had her hand on her hip and her head cocked to the side. She did that when she was trying to get information out of me. It was cute. "It was alright, just the average," I said, knowing I was lying through my teeth. "Hey just meet me at T.G.I Fridays at about noon." I told her trying to get myself together. "All right baby, see you there" she said before hanging up the phone. I put the phone on the hook, "I need to take a hot shower to wash this shit off me, and then I'll feel better." I said while taking off my shirt then heading to the bathroom.

It was about 11:50 am when I got to T.G.I Fridays. I always got to places early. This was something I learned from my father, who was an ex-marine. He wasn't the typical Marine. He wasn't the crazy, shoot'em guy that is usually described by most movies. He was cool minded and very sincere about mostly everything. Don't get me wrong; he would get in that ass when it was time. But most of the time my mom did the discipline because he was almost always gone on some type of mission or deployment. He died almost three years ago when I was in college. It hurt me so much; I didn't even want to go back to school. I just wanted to curl up and stop breathing. My dad was a great, great man. I wanted to be the man he was, but so far, I've come up short. But I always remember one thing he told me "son if you don't remember one thing that I tell you, remember this, a man can only be as good as he desires to be. When you become the man that you want to be, it will not be because of me, your mother, or the woman in your life, it is up to you". "I want to be a good man, pops, just like you," I said looking him in his eyes as he laid in the hospital bed. He had contracted lung cancer, but it was a kick in the chest from one of the horse's he had that put him in this state. "Don't be like me son, be better than me. Because if you're not, that means I didn't raise you right" he told me. That was the last conversation I had with my dad. I will never forget the most important man in my life. Never.

When Candy show up about 12:10 I was sitting at a booth. She came in and sat down across from me. "I see you got that big ass purse. You might as well get a back pack with the size of that thing" I said with a smile on my face "Shut up boy, you always got something to say, smart-ass" she joked back at me. I laughed and picked up the menu that the waitress had just dropped off when I first sat down. "So how was the drive baby?" I asked her. "The traffic wasn't that bad, hey you know who called me out the blue this morning?" she asked. "Who?" I asked. "Your girl Tasha" she said smiling. The waitress came over and asked us what we wanted to drink. "I'll take a root beer and she wants a strawberry lemonade." I told her. "You know me so well baby," Candy said looking at me like I was the best thing since sliced bread. The waitress left and I continue with our conversation. "Oh yeah, what she want?" I ask with a bad feeling in the pit of my throat. "She wants to go to church with me tomorrow. I think it's a good idea. I haven't seen her much since she got that new job at night. She won't ever tell me what it is. I just hope she ain't selling herself or nothing like that" she said with a laugh. I put on a small grin and replied "yeah, that wouldn't be good". "You're coming right?" she asked. We always went to church together. We did almost everything together. "There's a good game coming on tomorrow. I have to see if the Cowboys will make the play-offs," I said to her. But the real reason I didn't want to go was because of the sin I had committed last night. It would be too weird to be in church of all places with Candy and Tasha. "Ok baby, if you can't, you can't" she answered with a disappointed look on her face. I hated that look. I never wanted to make her feel bad or feel that I was choosing something else over her. I wanted her to know that she comes before everything I my life, everything.

The waitress came back with the drinks, and requested our orders. "I'll take the Jack Daniels ribs and shrimp and she will take" I said before Candy interrupted me. "I'll take the Jack Daniels Chicken". This was a change because she usually gets the shrimp. The waitress wrote it down, gave us a smile, and walked away. "No shrimp today" I asked Candy. "Knaw, just the chicken. I'm not in a fishy mood" she answered. We sat there quiet for some time. She was checking her text messages and I was playing around with a game on my phone. Then I broke the silence, "Ok, I'll go". "Good, I would feel better if you do. Tasha and I are close but we both have changed through the years. I want you to be nice too. I know you two had that thing back in the days, but I hope you two don't have anything against each other." "Baby, I don't have anything to do with that girl, that was college, I'm with you and I'm cool with anyone you want me to be. I just want to make you happy" I said. But that statement hurt worse than getting stabbed with a hot tipped poker. She can see it in my face. "What's wrong baby?" she asked with concern. "I'm just hungry" I replied, but it was a lie. I was so uncomfortable right now; I could have been sitting on a seat of nails.

The waitress came with the food. "Jack ribs and shrimp, and chicken, can I get you anything else?" she asked. "Knaw, we are cool, thank you miss" I replied. She put the check on the table and walked away. The food was steaming hot and smelled so good. I grab the slab and tore off a rib. I placed it in my mouth, it was cooked just right. It was soft with just the right amount of seasoning. I finished the rib and grabbed the shrimp. The shrimp was breaded and a good size. I dipped it in the Jack Daniels sauce and took a bite. The flavor was great and just enough sweetness to excite my taste buds.

We ate in silence. There was no time to talk when food was around. We both just dug in. When we finished Candy spoke. "That was very good. Thank you" "Baby, what I tell you about that, you don't have to thank me for nothing. You're my women. I got you." I said with a sly smile on my face. "Come here and give me some goodness," I told her while poking out my lips. She leaned over the table and kisses me gently on my lips, while holding my face with her left hand then sat back down. "You about to get me swolle up in here" I told her. "Well calm down, because I have to go" she said. When it came to sex with Candy, it wasn't going to happen anytime soon. Like I said, she was a good girl with morals. But it didn't help that I have a sexual drive that could power a 1969 Ford Mustang with no problem.

She told me that she wanted to wait until she was ready and I had no problem with that. I took out my cobra skin wallet and paid for the bill. Candy paid always paid the tip. We got up and walked out the restaurant. I held the door open for her and watched her walk by me. "Mmm, mmm, mmm" I said loudly as she walked by. "STOP IT!" she yelled at me with embarrassment. I walked her to her car. She had a little blue Ford Focus. I hated that car. It looked too bug like, but she loved it. We hugged each other, kissed, and parted ways.

When I returned home I felt better since I had a chance to spend some time with Candy. I unlocked the door, opened it and closed it behind me. I threw the keys on the table that sat right by the door. My apartment wasn't that big. It was a two bedroom, two baths. One bathroom was in the master bedrooms and other one was downstairs under the staircase in between the living room and kitchen. Both bedrooms were upstairs. I used the extra room as a gym/guess room. The guest room had a skiing machine, a bed, a TV, and some dumbbells. The bedroom I slept in had a king size bed, with a high headboard, plush pillows and a thick blue comforter. I had a 42-inch plasma hanging on the wall facing the foot of the bed and a red wood dresser set. Downstairs I had a big black sectional with a recliner at the end. A 52 inch TV hung on the wall in front of the sectional. In the kitchen area I had a four-chair wood kitchen table.

I went to the kitchen to get some apple juice. As I did, I saw the message button on the phone in the kitchen was blinking. I push the bright red button. "You have one new message" the machine spoke. "Say cuz, what you doing? I can't stop thinking about that freak last night. Hit me up." "Yep, leave it to Toni to remind me of something I didn't want to think about" I thought to myself. I put the phone on speaker mode and dialed his number. The phone rang as I took off my shoes. "Hello" it was his mother. "Hello Miss Johnson, is Toni home?" I asked her. "Yeah he in there, TONI, SAMMY IS ON THE PHONE!" she yelled. She sounded sexy as all get out on the phone. "WHAT UP CUZ?" Toni said taking the phone from his mom. "I'm chilling dawg, just came back from eating with Candy." I told him while scratching the bottom of my foot. "Yeah, did you feel all guilty and shit?" he asked. "Hell yeah, that was some fucked up shit we did" I said to him. "Hey, the bitch said she wasn't going to say anything cuz, stop trippin' over it" Toni replied. "Plus you know you liked it anyway" Toni added. "That ain't the point, if it was some girl we met at Fox Hills or Slauson, cool, but her BEST FRIEND! Come on man. But I'm done talking about it. What you going into today?" I said changing the subject. He whispered, "I have to go serve something, and drop off a package, then I'll get up with you later." "Alright man, I don't know why you don't just get a real job, and quit that hustling?" I asked. "I will cuz, I will. I'll holla." Toni replied. "Alright" I said then hung up the phone.

I spent the whole afternoon laying around the house watching sports and scratching my balls. If you didn't know, that's what guys do on the weekend. Sports had always been a big deal to me ever since I was a little boy. I remember I used to play basketball all the time by myself. I used to have to throw the basketball against the pole in the fence so I can have someone to pass to. I have two older sisters. Annie was seven years older than me, she lived in San Francisco, and Lonnie, who was three years older than I, and she was back in Mississippi. I was the baby boy. They had me doing all types of stuff when I was a kid. Playing with Barbie dolls, doing hair on cabbage patch kids, everyone swore I was going to grow up to be gay. But I think the experience gave me a jump on all the guys that didn't have this experience. I could relate to women on a different level other than trying to fuck. I listened to them. I cared about what they were saying. I cared about why they did what they do. To be totally honest with you, I enjoyed talking to females more than guys.

At about half time of the three o'clock college football game the phone rang. It was my sister Annie. She called me more than anyone in the family. I think it's because we are both in Cali. "Hey Annie, how are you doing?" I said to my sister. "Nothing much Ducky" she replied. That was the nick name that she gave me when I was a very young boy. She was the only one that called me that. I had a rubber ducky that I took around with me ever where I went. "Hey Ducky, I wanted to ask your opinion on something" she asked. Even though I was younger, my sister valued my advice on life. It did matter if it was on one of my three nieces or her dead beat ex-husband, she would ask me. "Shoot" I offered. "Well Stevie says that he misses home and misses the kids. I want to believe him, but I don't know. What do you think?" she asked. "Well hell, you the one that threw him out because he came home thirty minutes late from work!" I told her. "Well, he was cheating" she explained. "You think he was. Stevie has been the best cat out of the bunch and you do him like that. He works, takes care of the kids, and supplied you a place to live. You better leave that man alone." I said. "You're right, I'll call him and tell him to come on home. That's all I wanted. When you and Candy coming up?" My sister loved Candy. They had so much in common, and loved each other's company. "I'm off next weekend." I replied. "Alright Ducky, love you" my sister said. "Alright, kiss my nieces for me" I requested. "I will, bye" she replied. "Bye" I said as the phone hung up.

It was about 8:30 pm when I heard the doorbell ring. "It must be Toni," I thought. I opened the door and Toni fell onto the floor bleeding, beat up and bruised. "WHAT THE FUCK?" I yelled. As I looked out the door, a black Cadillac Escalade drive off so fast that it left tire marks on the road. "TONI, WHAT THE FUCK HAPPENED?" I said as I picked my friend up off the floor and closed the door. I sat him on the sectional. "Ain't nothing cuz, just part of the game, just part of the game" he replied. His voice was very weak. "Knaw dawg, what happened?" I demanded. "I was short five dollars, so they wanted to teach me a lesson, that's all cuz" he said wiping his bloody lip. His hand looked like it had been drugged through the street and back. "That's it man? That's some bullshit. We going to have to get you a real job or something. You're my dawg; I can't see you like this again. You hear me?" I pleaded with him. "Yeah cuz, whatever you say. I can't go home like this, moms would have a heart attack. Can I stay here?" he asked me. "Fo sho. You can sleep in the guest room. Here, let me get you something to drink." I said walking before walking to the kitchen. I opened the cabinet and pulled out a bottle of Hennessey and poured it into a small glass. I brought the bottle and a second glass with me and sat it on the coffee table. I handed him a glass and he took a sip. His hand was shaking as he held the glass in his hand. "I thought they was going to kill me cuz. All this for five mutha fucking dollars. I knew I shouldn't have fucked with them nigga's. I should go get those hoes cuz" he said with anger in his voice. "Knaw dawg, don't even think about it. I'm mad too dawg, but what can we do? Hell I could have given you five dollars." I said to him with my fist clutched tight. "I know cuz, but I can't get you involved in shit like this, you have a good thing going, and I don't want you fucking it up over me." Toni replied. "Yeah, that's how that business is. But damn. My cousin that was in Memphis, Tennessee was in the game DEEP. One day the guy around the block decided he wanted his clientele. He put two to the back of kin folk's head." I told Toni. "Did you do anything about it cuz?" Toni asked. I sat back in my sofa. "No, but that cat isn't breathing anymore though" I told him. "How you know that then cuz?" he asked. "Because my baby cousin is in prison serving time right now for knocking him down. My family is very tight, but we didn't win anything from it. You might as well say we lost two people we love, for one greedy mutha fucka, ya dig? I don't want to loss you. You're the only family I got out here besides my sister and nieces. I love you." I confessed to him. "Aw cuz, I love you too" he replied. We gave dap and the tender moment was interrupted by Beyoncé' on BET. "LOOK AT THAT ASS CUZ!" Toni yelled. "Fuck that, she ain't got shit on Trina" I contested. This was our daily argument. We laughed and drank all night. We forgot about him getting the shit beat out of him and me meeting up with Candy and Tasha tomorrow for church. Right now, the only thing that was on our minds was enjoying each other's company and drinking the world away. That's my friend.

CHAPTER FOUR
Uncomfortable situation

The next morning I awoke to find Toni sitting on the couch watching Looney Toons and eating Captain Crunch. I went in the kitchen to make me a bowl before getting ready for church. "Damn nigga, you just had to drink all the milk," I yelled at Toni. "Say homie, you only had a swallow anyway" he replied. "That's all right, I have some can milk" I thought to myself. I always kept can milk in the house in case I ran out of regular milk, plus I didn't mind using it because made the cereal that much sweeter. I took this idea from my mom. She would give us this milk for our cereal to save money. I popped two holes directly across from each other on the top of the can. This gave the can room to breathe, so the milk just flowed out. I pour some cereal in a big red bowl, and pour the milk on top. I put the milk in the refrigerator and placed the cereal on top of the icebox. I walked back in the living room wearing a tee shirt, boxers, and flip-flops. I sat down on the sofa and began eat my food. "Why you got to eat out of that dead ass bowl, cuz," he said referring to the color of my bowl. Red was the color affiliated with the blood gang in LA and major parts of America. Toni grew up in the neighborhood where Crips ran the streets, which wore blue and affiliated themselves with the color blue.

I don't do all that 'banging' stuff dawg, I'm a country boy, we don't roll like that," I told Toni as I kept eating. "Whatever" he mumbled to himself. "I'm going to get up out of here in a minute, I know you have a bit of a situation you have to deal with this morning. I don't even know why you going. Shit, I wouldn't go. Y'all going to set the church on fire with all that sin y'all have going on." Toni laughed. I had forgotten that Tasha was going to be at church also. "FUCK! With that stuff that happened last night, I forgot about that." I said as I jumped to my feet taking my bowl back in the kitchen. "YEAH CUZ! The shit is going to hit the fan. That bitch is going to get in the church and start feeling guilty. Then she is going to tell your girl everything. Good luck homie," Toni said while putting on his shoes then fixing his pants so they sag just right. "The only thing I ask is, can you give a nigga ride home?" he asked with a big grin on his face. "Man fuck you, you can walk. You got all that energy to talk that shit." I said in a joking way. "Just hurry your ass up, I don't want you to be late for you double date, ha." Toni laughed. I ran upstairs and put on the clothes I had laid out. It was an all blue silk-like dress shirt and black silk-like pants. I wore the shirt un-tucked. I thought it looked better that way. I had a Versace' belt that I only wore to church because it cost too much to wear anywhere else. I looked in the mirror, fixed my clothes, sprayed on some Curve cologne and went back down stairs. Toni waited by the door with my keys in his hands. "I can't wait to get the Cutlass fixed so I can dip out whenever I want, slow ass." Toni said handing me my keys. "Or you can ask them guys from last night to give you another ride" I said snatching the keys. "Fuck you" Toni replied.

When I got to the church it was 11:02. As I passed the front of the church a saw Candy and Tasha standing there watching my car as it passed. I parked my car, grabbed my bible out the glove compartment and got out the car. As I hit my alarm, Candy walked up on me fast. "Why are you late?" she asked pointing her finger in my face. "Hey, this is God's day, let's don't start off on a bad note." I replied to her. "You ready?" I asked her. She wrapped her right arm in my left arm and we walked towards the entrance of the church. Tasha stood there looking. "Long time no see Sammy" Tasha said to me holding her hand out. I grabbed her hand with my free right hand and shook it. "How have you been, Tasha?" I asked her. "Fine, let's get up in here before it gets started." Candy insisted.

As we entered the church, it was about half full. We sat in a middle row. I sat the end of seat, Candy sat to my right, and then Tasha on the other side of her. I never felt this uncomfortable in church in my life. The preacher didn't make it any better. His

sermon was about, 'fighting temptation to get what you desire'.
We put our heads down to pray. Candy always puts her head in
her lap when she prayed. When she did that a saw Tasha staring at
me out of the corner of her eye. I closed my eyes and tried to clear
my mind, but I could feel her eyes watching me from the side.
"Amen" we all spoke as the prayer finished. We gave tides and
offerings, and then the service was over.

After church we stood outside talking to the other members.
Candy was over in the grass area talking to Mrs. Tidwell. She was
an older lady that took a liking to Candy. They talk on the phone
about different things. Sometimes Candy would ask her advice on
life. I thought that was good that she had a "mother figure" out
here she could talk to. At that moment

I felt something brush against my booty. It was Tasha standing
next to me. "So what's going on playa? You still tired from the
other night?" she asked with a sly grin on her face. "Hey, don't be
doing that stuff out here, what's wrong with you?" I said harshly.
"Don't worry Sammy, it's all good. Candy will never know. And
if you want to do it again, she won't find out about that either.
You got some good shit down there," she said dropping her eyes to
my pants while biting her bottom lip, then looked up and let her lip
drop in a sexual way. "Tasha, yes I have to admit that I enjoyed
every minute of what we did, but it can't happen again. I can't do
Candy like that again. I can't," I pleaded. "Why not, she ain't
giving you any. You need to go ahead and break it off with Miss
Goody-goody" she replied with attitude. Then I notice that Candy
was glaring at us from a distance. I lowered my voice "Tasha, this
is not the place for this. Just know that we can't, and that's it.
Candy is coming, so stop it." Candy walked over. "Is everything
alright over here?" she asked both of us. "Yeah, we was just
talking about the Cowboys making it to the play-offs. Tasha says
that their not" I said quickly. Candy knew that Tasha loved
football because watching the football games with her father was
one of the only good memories she shared with him before he got
locked up. "Because they're not" Tasha added. She was smooth,

too damn smooth. "Oh, ok" Candy said with an unsure look on her face. "Hey, do you guys want to get something to eat?" Tasha asked. I didn't want to spend another minute in her presence. I feared she would say something, or hint to something that will make Candy mad or suspect something. "Knaw, its 12:45, the games should still be on. I'm going to try to catch the end of it." I said looking at the both of them. "Alright honey, I'll call you later. Thank you for coming" Candy said giving me a hug and a kiss on the cheek. "Yeah, bye HONEY!" Tasha said with a smirk looking back over her shoulder as they walked away. I squint my eyes at her and thought, "BITCH" in my head.

I stopped by my friend Ced's house on my way home. I met Ced in college. Ced was from South Carolina. He was an outstanding running back for USC that should have went pro but he messed up his knee in a car accident. Ced, another guy from the football team and I were coming back to campus after attending a house party in west LA. Then a drunk driver ran a red light and hit us from the side. His friend only had a bruised elbow and some scratches, I had an extreme headache but Ced tore his ACL. That night, Ced's dreams of being a professional athlete ended.

I pulled up to Ced's drive way and I notice that he had his car still running. I walked up to the door and rang the doorbell. The door was opened but the screen door was closed, so I could look inside. "What's up pimp? I'll be out in a minute." Ced called from the back of the house. Ced came out tucking in his shirt. Ced was about 6'2", broad shoulders, light brown completion and still had his athletic build. All the women loved his physique. He always cut his hair low with a fade "to kick the waves" as he like to say. "Where you going dawg?" I asked Ced. "Man I'm about to run to Tammy's house. The family is getting together to watch the afternoon game. Want to come?" Ced offered. "Hell yeah!" I replied. I liked going to his girl's house. Her family was from Mississippi also. They always took me in as family whenever I came over. No matter what, if there was any kind of sporting event going on, they always got together. Soul food, laughter, it was always a good time. Me and her dad Jeff would always get into it over football. I love the cowboys and he was a San Francisco fan. But it was all in good fun.

"Let's take your car," I said to Ced. He had a 1995 Chevy Impala that had money green candy paint and 20" rims on it. Brown leather interior and TV's in the sun visors. It was clean and he knew I love to ride in it. "Not today dawg, me and the ol' lady going to spend some "alone" time after the game. Get in you ragged shit and let's go" he said laughing as he jumped in the driver seat of his car. I gave him the middle finger then hoped back in my car. I backed out and let him go ahead of me. I hated following him. He would get all the looks from the females when we stopped at a stop light and I wouldn't get shit.

We found a parking spot on the street because the driveway was full with cars already. The house was a pale pink color with gates on the windows and a small metal fence around the house. The grass was green and lined with different types of flowers. When we walked up to the door, we could hear the game blasting through the screen door. We knocked and proceeded in. In the living room, her father sat in his usual recliner chair, her mother sat next to him on the sofa. Her little brother J.R. was on the floor and Tammy was in the kitchen. In the back yard was her uncle Billy Jean, which was visiting from Mississippi, with his two kids Jonathon and Lilly. Then there was another guy I had never seen before there too. Billy was at the bar-b-que pit. The smell of ribs, chicken and steak filled the house. "Hello boys, come on in and have a seat." Mr. Jones told us. Ced sat next to Tammy's mother and I grabbed a chair from the kitchen table and brought it into the living room. "How are you boy's doing?" Mrs. Jones asked us. "Fine ma'am" Ced and I both answered at the same time. With a sip of his beer Mr. Jones spoke "those Cowgirls about to get that ass handed to them" he said looking at me with a smile. "No sir, we already winning, look at the score" I replied. "One field goal isn't going to be enough to finish Minnesota" Mr. Jones debated. "He we go" Ced said to Mrs. Jones. "I know, I know, but Jeff loves this type of thing" she replied to Ced. Ced got up from the couch and went into the kitchen.

Tammy was a dark brown skinned just like the rest of the people in her family. She stood about 5'4" nice thick legs, wide child bearing hips and a nice round booty. Ced and I met her at Club Bee Real while we was in college. Her and her friends were on the dance floor working it. All the California guys were intimidated by it but I had that hen and coke in me and Ced was drinking that straight "yac" so we decided to hit the dance floor. We waited for the right song to play and it was Lil Keke's "South Side". We got on the dance floor and started doing the "South Side" dance. "Oh snap, we got some country boys in the house!" one of Tammy's friends said with excitement. Then the song changed up to Juvenile's song "Back That Ass Up" and then the party was on. Tammy backed it up on Ced, and the loud mouth friend got on me. She thought she could break me off, but I guess she didn't know who she was dealing with. I put it on her so bad, grinding, sliding, rubbing, snaking that she was totally sweating after the song was over. We went back to the table after the song, talked, exchanged numbers and Tammy and Ced have been together ever since. That's been two years now. As for me and the friend, which her name was Tametra, we talked for two weeks, had sex and that was it. All that dancing she was doing and she couldn't even ride dick right, amazing.

Tammy and Ced came out of the kitchen. I always liked seeing them together. This kept hope in my mind that there is someone in the world for everyone. "Hey Sexy Sammy" she said to me joking. She always called me that because she told me once that I think that I'm the sexiest guy on earth. I thought that it was funny because I didn't carry myself in that manner if you ask me. "Hey Tammy, where your girl Tametra at?" I said laughing. "Oh don't start, you know she live right down the street. She got a new man now. And I don't think he would like it if you go sniffing around. Plus you had your chance" she said to me pointing her finger and rolling her neck. "I'll take his chick if I want too. Plus I was kidding anyway, LAME!" I told her laughing. Ced started laugh because he knew what I was talking about. Tammy elbowed him and gave him a serious look. He just smiled and put his hands in the air with the "what?" expression on his face. "I'm sorry Tammy. Sorry that your friend is LAME!" I said again. Tammy ran over to me and put me in the headlock. Her little brother jumped up, grabbed my arm and playfully bit it. "Y'ALL QUIT THAT PLAYING IN THIS HOUSE TAMMY!" Mrs. Jones yelled. "Sorry momma" Tammy and J.R. spoke. "Sorry momma" I said as I went over to hug her. "Get off me boy" Mrs. Jones told me smiling. I sat back down in my chair. We watched the game, ate, and laughed. The Cowboy's won the game so I had a lot of ammunition the next time Mr. Jones and I spoke.

It was 8:00 pm when I felt my cell phone vibrate in my pocket. "Hello" I said answering the phone. It was Tasha. "Is this a bad time?" she asked. "Hold on" I told her. "Hey Ced. I'm about to roll out dawg." I said to Ced. "Alright pimp, tell Candy I said what's up," he said winking at me. I gave him the middle finger. I shook Mr. Jones hand with a grin on my face. He gave me no reply. I hugged Mrs. Jones, hugged Tammy and pushed her shoulder when I let her go. "Hey boy" she said as she got in a fight position, then I slapped her little brother gently on the head. Then I ran out the door.

When I got out side I resumed talking to Tasha. "Why are you calling me?" I asked. "See, I don't even know why you tripping. I just wanted to ask you for your boy, um, what was his name?" she asked. "Toni" I replied as I got in the car, closed the door and turn the ignition key. The car sounded like it needed a tune up. "I'll get one before I go to San Fran" I thought to myself. "Yeah, what's his number?" she asked. "Well is this your number on the caller id?' I asked her. "Yeah, why" she replied. "Because I don't give out his number, so I'll have him call you." I informed her. I didn't want to say the real reason, that he stayed with his mother and she 'don't like everybody calling her house' as she would say. "Oh, well that's ok, never mind" she said with uncertainness in her voice. "Ok Tasha, I have to go. I'll," I said before she cut in. "Is it like that? You can't talk to a sista anymore?" she asked. "I don't think it would be good for the situation that I'm in" I told her. "Well I told you that everything is on the DL. Why you tripping? I just want a little taste, that's all" she confessed.

As I was going to make the last left to my apartment I told her "well I can't because I already feel guilty and I'm almost home." With anger in her voice she told me "oh she got you tied huh? So you going to act like a little bitch and not give me the dick?" "Tasha she is your friend, how can you be like that to your friend?" I asked her before parking in my parking spot and turning off the car. "Friend is one thing, some good dick is another" she replied. "Ok, I'll go get my dawg and y'all can handle it" I said trying to give her an alternative. "That's ok, but just tell me this before I hang up. If the situation was different, would I get the dick again?" she asked. I sat for a minute, thought about it and answered "yes, I would do it again, hold on" my phone was beeping. "Hello" I said as I clicked over. "Hey honey, what are you doing?" Candy asked. "On the phone with Toni, he was asking me if you knew any girls. I told him about Tasha." I replied to her. "Oh yeah? She is single. Did you tell him about that nice ass she got?" she said in a joking manner. "I don't know nothing about that," I answered. "Don't act like you don't know," she said to me. "Hold on baby" I said as I clicked back over. "Is that another tramp that wants to get with you?" Tasha asked in a jealous way. "NO! Its Candy, I have to go." I told her in a harsh tone. "Alright good looking. Don't forget about these lips while you're dreaming." Tasha said before I heard a click from her phone. "I'm back baby." I said after clicking back over. I got out of the car, hit the alarm button and walked towards my door. As I did, I saw the black Cadillac truck from last night up the street.

When I got to the door, it slowly drove off. "Yeah baby, I just want to know if you wanted me to come over?" she asked me. When she came over it was the same thing. She would come over, cuddle with me until my dick got hard and then tell me she wasn't ready. But I figure I better let her come over because with that truck being out there, I didn't want to be alone. "Yeah baby. I would like that." I said to her in a loving way. "Alright, I'll be right over" she said. "Alright baby, I'll be waiting" I said before I put the phone in my pocket and went in the apartment.

Candy came over about 10:00. I don't know why she wanted to come over so late. She knew I had to get up for work at 5:00 am to be ready to leave the house about 6. I had to be at work at 7:00 am that's why I left at 6 because like I said before, LA traffic will get crazy. She didn't have to be at her first class until 9:00 am. So she would stay and clean up a little before she left. I think she gets tired of her roommates some times. They would have their boyfriends running in and out of the apartment. It made her feel uncomfortable.

We laid in the bed watching TV. I was behind her in the spoon position. She liked to be held. It made her feel secure. I hated it, because her nice round, firm ass would be on my dick, and my manhood would start to grow with any little movement that she would make. "You so bad" she would say. But tonight was different. My mind kept rolling back to the conversation that I had with Tasha and the black truck outside. I didn't tell Candy about last night because all she would do is worry. As I was thinking about that, I fell asleep. I woke up to see that the TV was off and Candy was dead asleep on the other side of the bed under the covers. I got up and walked to the bathroom to pee. I pulled up the toilet seat and started to pee. I was a good release. When I finished, I shook my dick; put the seat back down and went back to bed.

CHAPTER FIVE
I've never felt love like this before

Three months had passed and everything was going good. I have gotten Toni a job at my company in the mailroom. He liked the fact that he could listen to his headphones all day and hardly be bothered. Candy and I were still kicking it strong. Even though the sex part of our relationship hadn't come yet, I can say now that I love this woman. I hadn't heard much from Tasha since the night that she called me on the phone. I would see her from time to time with Candy but nothing more than that. She looked a little down and out the last time they were together. She wasn't the same spirited young lady that I recognized. She seems to have something burdening her. Ced finally popped the question to Tammy. The wedding was going to be in the summer time. Ced had saved up for a honeymoon in Jamaica. I was very surprised at the fact that Ced bought her such a big diamond ring. He usually didn't spend much money on no one but himself. That's when I knew he really loved her. Ced asked me to be his best man and was very honored.

I was headed down to Hollywood suit outlet to see what they had to offer for suits. I was doing the research for Ced because he didn't have much time to do it himself, plus he always said I had a better sense of style than he did. "Give me some jeans, jersey, and some Air Force One's and I'm straight," Ced would always tell me when we would go shopping at Fox hills mall.

I hated driving down to the suit outlet. There was never any free parking. I drove around until I gave up and I parked at the first open meter I could find, put five dollar worth of quarters in the machine and walked to the suit outlet. I was looking through the suits to my surprise I saw that FUBU made tuxedos. They looked a little different from the other ones, so I took note of that in my palm pilot. I checked out some stuff for me, and then I went back to the car. I hit the alarm, open the door and sat down with the door open.

I checked my palm pilot to make sure I wrote down the right information. Out of the blue I saw a shadow on the outside of my door. I looked up quick with a "what the fuck" look on my face and to my surprise it was Shadow from Slauson. "What's going on girl?" I asked her with a big smile on my face. "Nothing much. I saw you walking down the street and decided to speak" she answered. "I can't believe you remember me. As good as you look, you must have a gang of cats hollering at you" I said with surprise. "I don't mean to toot my own horn but, WWHHOOO, WWHHOO" she said with a laugh. "Knaw, I just couldn't forget the way I felt when you and your friend talked to us. Jazmin and I wondered why you guys never called. Y'all must have found some coochie after the club" she added. She didn't know how right she was. "Knaw Miss Lady, we just chilled" I said to her. "So what brings you down here?" I asked her. "Just window shopping for shoes" she replied. "Cool, I hate to cut it short, but I have to get away from this meter. You got a ride?" I asked her. "No, I caught the bus down here" she replied. "Well hop on in, I'll give you a ride" I offered. "Thanks" she said then she walked around the car to the passenger side. Her body was still banging. She had that confident walk that I always loved for a woman to have. She had on some black Capri pants with a white tee shirt and some running shoes. Even being dressed down she still could turn every straight man's head, and some gay. I unlocked the passenger door and she got in. She smelled so sweet and her hair was freshly done. While we drove, I kept peeking at her thighs out of the corner of my eye.

Our conversation during the drive was great. She finally told me her real name was Tonia. She liked a lot of the things I liked. We both enjoyed watching movies, writing, and cars. She was very surprised to learn that I get manicures and pedicures. She told me that she wanted to see that for herself and would even pay for it. I didn't mind that at all. I told her about Candy and how much I was digging her and to my surprise she understood. Tonia was a delight to talk to. When we reached her mother's house in Lynwood she looked at me and said "I really enjoyed talking to you and thank you for the ride". "My pleasure, I really enjoyed your company too." I replied to her. Then she suddenly kissed me on my lips opened the door and ran into the house. When she got to the door she turned around and waved. I waved back and drove off.

I drove home thinking to myself "she sure was nice and that body was banging. I should try to beat. I still had the number in my palm pilot, plus I haven't had sex since that night with Tasha." When I got to my parking spot at my apartment I heard my phone ring. "Hello" I answered. "Say cuz, where you at?" Toni asked. "I just pulled into the crib. Why what's up?" I asked him. "Just wanted to know if you was still out looking for those tuxes for the wedding?" he asked. "Knaw I'm done with that. OH! Guess who I saw down in Hollywood when I was there?" I asked him. "Who?" Toni replied. "Remember that time we was at Slauson and we ran into those two fine bitches?" I asked him. "Yeah, Jazmin and that Shadow bitch that didn't want to tell us her name" he replied. "Well Shadow's real name is Tonia and that bitch is still fine." I told him with an excited voice. "Fo real? So what happened cuz?" Toni asked me. "Well she walked up on my car and almost got knocked the fuck out because I wasn't paying attention and she just popped up. So we started talking, I took her home, the bitch kissed me and ran in the house like some little girl or something." I told Toni. "Well hell, does that even matter?" Toni asked me. "True, true" I replied. "I thought about trying to fuck, but I don't want to be that cheating cat that gets caught up in the end." I admitted to him. "MAN, FUCK ALL THAT CUZ! You only twenty-six years old. You needs to fuck as many bitches you can before Candy tie your ass down, fo real cuz" Toni said to me. "Yeah, but" I said before he cut me off. "Have you had sex with Candy?" he asked. "Well" I said before he cut me off again. "Have you had sex with Candy?" he asked again. "No, but she isn't like that." I told Toni. "I know cuz, but you're a man. You have a dick and some balls that need special attention. If she isn't someone has to. You don't have to leave her because she is a good girl, I know that, but DAMN NIGGA! You haven't fucked anyone since that bitch Tasha. Hell we need to call her back up," he said with a laugh. "Shit, she sucked my dick real good cuz." he added. I couldn't do anything but laugh. "She did do that dawg. My dick got hard last night thinking about that bomb head" I said to him. "You still got them Slauson bitches number?" Toni asked me. "Yeah, it's here in my palm pilot. You know what, tomorrow is Friday, I'll call her then. Candy is coming over tonight." I told Toni. "You a better man then me cuz. She couldn't be all in my crib, all in my bed and not give me anything. You a sappy ass nigga. You make it hard for real 'G's' like me" Toni said with a laugh. "Well I have to get in the house and cook 'G', I'll hit you up later" I said to him. "All right cuz, stay up" he said before hanging up the phone.

I went in the house and went straight to the kitchen. I pulled out a frozen, just add chicken stir-fry package out the freezer. I also took out the frozen egg rolls. I had two hours until Candy would be over. For some reason Candy really loved to eat this food. I'm more of a beans and cornbread type of guy myself.

I pulled out a skillet for the stir-fry. I put the skillet on the burner and set the knob to 350 degrees. I poured a little oil into the skillet. While it warmed up, I ran upstairs to get out of my clothes. We weren't going to do anything but sit at the house, eat and watch TV. I took everything off except my wife beater and my boxers. I slipped on my favorite slippers and ran back down stairs. I took the chicken out of the refrigerator along with a small bottle of apple juice. I opened the bottle of apple juice and took a long, deep drink. It was very refreshing going down my throat. I added the chicken to the skillet that I had already sliced up. After the chicken was done I opened the package and poured the contents in the skillet and cover it. It was going to take about twenty minutes for it to cook so I started the egg rolls. I put the egg rolls in the oven, set the knob to 400 degrees. "This should take about ten to twelve min," I said to myself. So I went in to the living room and started watching Sponge Bob Square pants. Ten minutes later I went into the kitchen to check on the egg rolls. They were done, so I took them out and turn off the oven. I put a plate over the pan and went back to the living room to watch TV. After another ten minutes I checked on the stir fry and it was done. I removed the skillet from the burner and turn the oven off.

By the time Candy came over I was watching "106 and Park" on BET. She rang the doorbell. I went to the door and opened it a crack. "Who is it?" I asked like I didn't know who it was. "Boy quit playing" she contested. I opened the door and let her in. She wore a tan sun dress with sun flowers all over it that came up right above the knee. When she walked by and all I could see was her booty move back and forth under her dress. "Why she be playing with me?" I thought to myself. She had a black Nike sports bag with her. I guess she knew she was going to spend the night.

She took her bag upstairs, I sat back on the couch and continued watching TV. She came down stairs, gave me a kiss and sat next to me. "Dinners done baby" I told her. "Good, because I am so hungry" she said before getting up and going to the kitchen. "Baby, do you want me to make your plate?" she called out to me. "Yes ma'am" I said back to her. "I AIN'T OLD!" she yelled. "Yeah, but I have to be nice to the help" I said with a laugh. Candy laughed "OH, I'M THE HELP! Alright nigga". She came back with both our plates. "Thank you baby" I said to her after she gave me my plate and we began to eat. I loved when she came over, I felt so complete. "This so good baby" she said to me. "So how are the roommates?" I asked her. "The same, wilding out. I don't understand where they get the energy from" she explained to me. "Hey, they are just being the typical college girls. They will grow up one day." I told her. "Yeah, you probably want me to be all wild like that, huh?" she asked while cutting her eyes at me. "Yeah, I want you to jump on my face with your pussy and get to pumping right now." I said to her smiling real big. I was joking, but if she did, hell I wouldn't mind at all. "If I did for real, you probably wouldn't know what to do next." she said with a smirk on her face. "You're probably right. I probably just sit there." I replied to her laughing. She got up and grabbed my plate to take them back to the kitchen. When she did, the dress had moved into her booty crack. I yelled out "IS THAT A THONG, IS THAT A THONG?" while waving my hands like Martin Lawrence did in that movie. "Boy you crazy" she said to me switching her ass hard trying to get it out. "I'll get that for you" I said then ran to her. "Boy quit" she said while giggling. When I got to her she was already in the kitchen. I got one knee and gently slid the dress out the crack of her ass. "Thank you. You can get up now" she said to me while she put the plates in the sink. "I think I like it down here" I said to her in a sexual way. She turned to me and said "what you mean by that?" "I mean, I wouldn't mind putting my head up under this dress right now." I said to her looking up into her eyes. "Really?" she asked. "Yeah" I said back. I bent down a little bit a put my head under her dress. She smells so good down there. I kiss her through her panties on the spot that I have wanted to touch since we met at the coffee shop. I gave it one more kiss the exact same way. I started running my hands up both her thighs until I got to the panty strings. When I started to pull them down she stopped me "ok baby, that's enough of that" then pushed my head away.

She walked back in the living room. I stayed in the kitchen with the "I can't believe this shit" look on my face. "BABY!" she called to me. I got up slow with my head feeling so hot that I could have been a volcano ready to erupt at that moment. I sat on the couch next to her and crossed my arms. "Baby, don't be mad, I'm sorry. I just" she said before I interrupted her. "You just can't bring yourself to do it, I know" I said to her with harshness to my voice. "You don't understand" she said with tears in her eyes. Then she got up and ran upstairs. I laid back on the couch and began watching TV. "I'm tired of this bull shit. Every muthafucking time. This shit is getting really old." I said to myself.

I heard her crying upstairs. "MAN, FUCK!" I said to myself. I sat up on the couch for a second, I got up and went upstairs. She heard me coming upstairs. "Leave me alone Sammy," she cried. When I came through the door I could see her lying on the bed. "Baby, we have been together more than three months now. I think I deserve some kind of explanation about what's going on with you" I demanded. She sat up on the bed holding a pillow. "Ok. Ok. Remember when I told you that I transferred from UCLA because of my teacher?" she asked me. "Yeah" I said before sitting down on the bed. "Well he tried hitting on me and I turned him down. Then he started following me around everywhere I went. I'm not just talking about at the school, in the mall, at the beauty salon, and everywhere else. So one day I confronted him in front of my apartment. I told him to leave me alone or I was going to the police. He got furious and told me I wasn't going to tell anyone. He grabbed me and dragged me into the apartment. He held me down and started kissing me, snatching at my clothes." she said fighting back the tears. "Aw baby!" I said silently. She continued "I had a dress on so he pulled it up and tried to take my panties off. At that moment I scratched his eyes and kicked him in the balls. I got the phone and called the police. While I was on the phone he ran off." "Does he still work there?" I asked her. "Yeah, the school dropped it, and made it like I was the bad guy. So that's when I transferred" she said holding the pillow tightly. I wanted to find this guy and fuck him up. But that wouldn't solve anything right now.

I crawled over to her and gave her a big hug. "Baby, I'm sssssooooo sorry baby. I didn't know and I was very selfish. I will never act like this towards you again." I said to her holding her. "It's alright honey, I should have told you a long time ago. I just didn't want anything to change between us. Some guys get chased away when they hear something like that." she replied while wiping the tears from her face. I grabbed her hand with my left hand and softly wiped the left eye with my right thumb. We looked into each other's eyes and in that moment I knew I would love this woman forever.

As we look into each other eyes I felt her slowly move towards me. Her eye's slowly closed and her lips met with mine. The feeling of the kiss had more feelings in it than any other kiss I have received in my life. It was so pure and innocent. I kissed her back with the same innocence. Then I felt her hands running up my chest to my neck. I leaned back from the kiss, took my hands and rubbed them gently on her face. She grabbed my right hand and began kissing the palm of it. Her eyes went from fright, to unsure, to sexual. Then out of nowhere she thrust her face at my face, kissing me so passionately.

She began to pull my shirt over my head when I stopped her and said "baby, are you sure you want to do this?" "Yes baby, I do" she replied before biting her bottom lip. We began kissing with so much heat and passion. My manhood had become stiffen and large that it peeked out the hole of my boxers. She took her hand a grabbed at my erection. "Mmmmmm" she moaned with my lips still on her mouth. The vibration tickled my nose.

I kissed her cheek and then kissed her neck. I sucked her neck while running my hands on her back with up and down strokes. She pushed me back and pulled her dress over her head. Her body looked that much better without clothes. I felt myself get harder than I was before. She didn't have a bra on. The 36c breasts were shapely and perky. I lunged forward putting the left one in my mouth while playing with other one with my right hand. They felt so soft in my hand and mouth. I used my tongue to make circles around her nipple and then I move to the right one, doing the same thing I did to the left one.

I took the breast out my mouth, grabbed her, lifted her up by grabbing her right below her booty and laid her down on the bed. I went down to her feet. I grabbed her left foot and placed her toes in my mouth. I began licking and sucking her toes. Then I did the same to her other foot. When I was done with that, I took both her ankles in each of my hands and slowly placed her feet on the bed with her knees bent. I leaned down and forward before parting her legs. I stood up, took her right leg and straightened it out. I looked at her before I started kissing her inner ankle. I slowly started kissing down her right leg like I was a shark after my prey. She squirmed slowly with pleasure.

When I got to her thighs I kissed and sucked both her inner thighs gently. She spread her legs open more, like she was telling me "come and get it." I slid off her thong and I moved up to her pussy and with one long wet lick of the tongue I spread her lips then one more slow, long lick to expose what I really need to get at, her clit. I licked her clit once and her body shifted. Then I placed it in my lips and licked it with the tip of my tongue at the same time. She began rubbing my head with her hands. "Oh shit," she said before taking her hands off my head and began rubbing her breast. I licked all around her pussy walls, making sure all the wetness got around. Then I stuck my tongue as far as it could go in her hole while flicking my tongue up and down. "Oh yeah, I like that baby" she said to me. With a mouth full of pussy I replied, "Yeah, you like this? I asked her. "Un huh, do it baby" she replied. I fucked her with my tongue for a minute then I went back to the clit and began sucking it some more. "Oh yeah baby, oh yeah, shit" she said to me. "RIGHT THERE, OH YEAH IM ABOUT TO" she yelled then she covered her face with a pillow. "YES!" she yelled with a muffled scream from the pillow. The creamy white cum began to run down her pussy and then she tried to push my head away because it was too sensitive down there but I pushed forward and kept licking. It must have been too much for her because she slid her body away from me "WHOA BOY! That was too much" she told me with a big smile on her face. "Yeah?" I said to her before walking to the bathroom. "Where do you think you're going?" she asked me. "To wash my mouth out and go back down stairs," I replied to her. "Well I see someone isn't ready to leave" she said referring to my dick that was sticking straight out the hole in front of my boxers. "You are right about that." I said looking down. "Come here" she said to me with her index finger directing me to come to her. I walked over to her and she sat on the side of the bed.

When I got to her she took my manhood into her hands and rubbed it back and forth. "I like this, I like this a lot," she said before placing me in her mouth. Her mouth felt so good. Her nice full lips were soft on the side of my dick. Her mouth wrapped tight around me. The inside of her mouth was wet and warm. Her head slid back and forth on my dick in a nice rhythm. She took my dick out of her mouth, licked around the tip and placed tit back in. "Oh shit baby," I said to her. Then she took me out of mouth, laid back on the bed and pulled my dick towards her pussy. "Be gentle, it's been a while." she said to me. "I will baby, you don't have to worry about that." I replied to her. She was hanging off the bed in a way that her feet were flat on the ground. I opened the drawer by the side of the bed and pulled out the condom with the gold wrapper. I slid it on me then I took off my boxers and wife beater. I got on my knees in between her legs. I let her guide me into her. Her pussy was so tight that I didn't know if I was going to cum on the way in. Inch by inch I went into her. Her body was very tense and she didn't make a sound at all. I didn't know if I wanted to continue, but I did. She was quite warm and very wet. I finally got all the way in. I slid it back nice and slow, then forward, then back, the forward until I felt her body began to relax. "Ok, I think I'm ready" she said to me with her eyes closed and arms crossed in front of her chest. I started going a little faster with the back and forth motion. I could feel that her thighs were tense, so I stayed at the speed. I kept going at that speed until I felt her legs relax. So I started to speed up a little bit then she uncrossed her arms, leaned forward slightly and put her hands on my shoulders. I took her right hand off my shoulder and placed her index finger in my mouth. She took it out of my mouth then put it in her mouth and started sucking it. About that time I could feel her water really start to flow more. She took her finger out of her mouth, "yes baby, stroke it like that, oh shit yeah," she told me. So I grabbed her legs, threw them over my shoulders and picked her up. "DAMN baby, like that?" she asked me. "Yeah, like this" I said before sliding her up and down on my dick while standing up. After about ten pumps I laid her back on the bed in the middle.

Still with her legs over my shoulders I started sliding my dick in with long, deep strokes. I did this for two reasons, one to make her feel good, and two so I wouldn't cum. "Stroke it baby, stroke it" she said to me. "You like it like that?" I asked her. "Yeah, but give it to me faster. I want you to cum all in me." "Alright" I replied to her. I took her legs off my shoulders and started stroking it fast, then faster, and then as fast as I could. She wrapped her legs around me and screamed "YES BABY, YES GIVE IT TO ME, GIVE ME THAT DICK!" I was gripping the covers with my hands so hard that the fitting sheet slid off. The muscles in my arms were tight and budging. She rubbed her hands up and down them. "OH YEAH BABY, I'M ABOUT TO CUM AGAIN, OH SHIT!" she screamed.

She put the pillow over her face to keep her screams down. I didn't care about how loud she was, as long as it was feeling good. I took the pillow off her face and threw it to the floor. I wanted to see her face as she came on my dick. I felt my love charging. It was such a wonderful feeling that I held her close as we both came. It was like a pleasure shock wave going through both of our bodies. We both laid there holding each other trying not to move because with every motion sent a sensational chill up both our spines. We didn't care about the sweat or being uncovered, all we cared about was both of us in this moment. I felt her begin to cry while in my arms and when she looked up at me I had tears in my eyes. She kissed my tears and we fell to sleep in that very spot. The last thought in my head was "If this is what love feels like, I've never felt love before.

CHAPTER SIX
I just hope she comes back to me

The next day was cold and rainy, which was a good thing. I could just lay in the bed with Candy all day and not do anything because I had the day off and she didn't have class. I woke up about 8:30 am. I walked down stairs with nothing but my boxers on. I went into the kitchen and walked over to the refrigerator. I opened it up and pulled out some eggs, shredded cheese, onions, ham slices and canned biscuits and began making omelets. Candy really enjoyed omelets. I cracked six eggs into a bowl and mixed them together. I cut the onions and ham slices into tiny squares. I opened the canned biscuits, put them into a round pan and then put them in the oven. I pour have the eggs into a skillet and cooked them until it looked almost fully cooked. I added the cheese, onions and ham that I had cut into small cubes onto the eggs and flipped it.

About that time Candy came down stairs wearing one of my football jerseys. Her hair was wild: it looked like she had been in a fight with a blow dryer and the blow dryer won. She walked over to me and tried to give me a kiss. I leaned back with my hand over my nose and said "did you brush your teeth?" She gave me a big smile and replied "don't even go there, your breath probably smells worse than mine". "Only if your coochie stank" I replied back to her before giving her a big kiss on the cheek. "You always got something smart to say" she said to me. "But you like it" I replied.

I finished making the omelets and the biscuits had finished also. Candy went into the living room and began watching TV. I made our plates, went into the refrigerator, got the orange juice out, poured us some orange juice then took Candy her plate. "Thank you baby, you're too good to me" she told me as she gave me a kiss on the cheek. I returned to the kitchen to get my plate when the phone rang. I looked at the caller id and it was Tasha. "Now what in the hell do she want?" I asked myself. I didn't want to seem suspicious so I answered the phone. "Hello" I said. "Sammy, is Candy over there?" she asked me. I replied, "Yeah, do you want to speak to her?" "No, I need to talk to you, it's very important" she replied to me with urgency in her voice. I thought about it for a second, then I replied "alright, I'll meet you at that park we met at when we were in college at two" I said to her quietly. "Alright, I'll be there" she said before hanging up the phone. I walked back to the living room with my plate and my glass of orange juice. "Who was that?" Candy asked me. "Aw, it wasn't anybody but Toni I have to meet him at two" I replied to her.

Candy turned off the TV and turned to me. "Ok Sammy, I want to talk about last night" she said to me. "Is there something wrong baby?" I asked her. "No, nothing wrong, I just want to get some stuff off my chest. You waited a long time for what we did and I appreciate it. Most men would have been gone a long time ago" she said to me with tears in her eyes. "Last night told me the answer to the questions that I have been asking myself since we met in the coffee shop. Could I love him? Is he a good man? Can I totally open myself to him? And all the answers to those questions are yes. Yes I love you, yes you're a good man, and yes I can totally open myself to him" she told me. Her statements hit me hard, right to my soul. I didn't know what to say or do. All I thought to myself was that I loved this woman more right now than any other time since we have known each other. I grabbed her hands and faced her. "Baby, I have loved you since I met you on the net. You mean more to me than anything in my life. You make me the man I am and I appreciate you" I said to her with tears in my eyes. When she saw the tears she wrapped me tight with her arms. I held her tight to me; I didn't want to let her go. She was mine and I was hers.

At about noon Candy headed upstairs to get some more rest. I took me a shower and got dressed in some grey sweat pants, an oversized tee shirt, and some Nike running shoes. I jumped in my car and headed off to see what Tasha had to say. "Maybe I should have told Candy the truth about what happened and start off with a clean slate. I don't think she would ever trust me, plus that's her best friend, no, I'll just keep it to myself" I thought to myself as I drove.

When I pulled up to the park about 1:40 pm and Tasha was already there sitting on the hood of her car. I parked on the other side of the street and walked over to her. "What's going on lady?" I asked her. She had a worried look on her face. "Tasha, what's wrong?" I asked her with a concerned tone. She looked up at me with a tear running down her right cheek. "I don't know how to say it Sammy" she said to me but looking away. "Tasha, it's all right, just what you have to say," I told her. "Sammy" she said before pausing. With her voice cracking she continued "Sammy, I'm pregnant". "Really, what's the big" I said before thinking about it. "Oh no, no, no, no, HELL NO! Are you sure?" I asked. "Yes Sammy, I went to the doctor's office a week ago. I'm three months." she said holding herself with her arms looking down. I gave her a hug. "The thing is, two weeks before and three weeks after you, me and Toni did what we did I hadn't been with anyone. So it might be yours or Toni's." she said wiping her eye still in my arms. I let her go and sat down on the sidewalk. I put my head in my hands. "How can the best day of my life become the worse day of my life?" I asked myself. "So me or Toni can be the daddy? Great, he is going to love this" I said to her. "I knew I shouldn't have" I said before stopping myself. I couldn't blame her for what happened. I wanted to do it and chose not to use protection. "Sammy, please don't be angry with me," she said starting to cry. I got up off the ground and hugged her again. I could tell that she was scared and sorry for what she had done. "So what we going to do?" I asked her. "I can't get rid of it. It's against my religion plus I'm too far along. That's why it's so hard. I know you and Candy are together and I don't want to mess up things with her. I love her." she said to me backing up. "I was afraid to tell you, I thought you would beat my ass or something." she said to me turning away from me. "I wish I had a good man like you in my life" she added. "Tasha, to tell you the truth and don't take this the wrong way, but this isn't about me, you or Toni, it's about that baby. When can we find out who is the daddy?" I asked her. "Not until the baby is born" she replied. "OH GREAT!" I yelled throwing my hands in the air walking towards my car. "I have to tell Toni, and Candy" I told her. "You don't have to tell her, I don't want her to know, she doesn't need to know." she said to me grabbing my arm and turning me around. "Yes she does. I'm sorry, but she needs to know and I'm telling her," I said yanking my arm away from her. "Sammy please" she said dropping to her knees. I turned around breathing deep. "Tasha, we can't keep this a secret. This is not like cheating on a math test. There are a lot of people's lives involved here. Listen, everything is going to be ok, but it's going to be terrible right now. I love Candy and I can't lie to her. It will hurt her more to find out in the future than to let her know now. But I have to go" I told her before picking her up off her knees and sitting her on her car hood. "Your right, that girl is going to kick my ass." she said trying to smile. "Not before she kicks mines, but go home and be careful," I said to her walking towards my car.

I got in my car and sat there for about fifteen minutes. "I better call Toni." I thought. I picked up my cell phone and dialed his number. The phone rang and rang. I hung up the phone and dialed again. After three rings he picked up. "WHAT CUZ!" he yelled. "What you doing dawg?" I asked him. "I'm fucking this bitch, what's up?" he asked. "Well tell that bitch to wait, I got some serious shit to tell you," I told him. "All right cuz, hold on" he replied. I heard him in the background telling the girl that she had to go. His mom must be gone for the weekend. She would go to Vegas every once in a while with one of her boyfriends. That's the only time he would bring a girl over to the house. "Alright cuz, I have to thank you. That bitch was lame. She couldn't give head, pussy was garbage. We need to call up Tasha for round two cuz, fo real." he said to me. "Well dawg, it's funny that you mentioned her name. I just got done talking to her right now." I replied. "Oh yeah? You set that up, because I'm ready tonight!" he said with a laugh. "Dawg, I hope your sitting down" I said to him. "What's going on cuz, she don't have AIDS or something do she," he asked with a little anger in his voice. "Knaw dawg, she's pregnant and it's either mines or yours" I told him. The phone was real quiet from a minute. "How she knows it was us? She works at the hole in the wall club where they sell ass and shit. Knaw, that baby ain't ours, fuck that, fuck that." he said to me. But it sounded like he was trying to convince himself. "You got a point, but I have to do something I don't want to do" I said to him. "I KNOW YOU ARE NOT GOING TO TELL CANDY! HELL KNAW!" he yelled. "I have to, because what if?" I told him. "WHAT IF, WHAT? Don't mess up your relationship for no hoe man. And that's what she is, a big hoe." he said to me. "Yeah, but what if she starts acting up? I rather me tell Candy now than her finding out in a fit of rage. Then she will ask me why I didn't tell her when I found out. If it's going to end, it's going end this way. And it's fucked up, I know I love her and plus we just had sex last night." I told Toni. "WHAT? That's so fucked up. Was it good?" Toni asked. "This ain't the time Toni. Hey, I'm about to go, I'll holla at you later on" I said to him. "Alright cuz, good luck" Toni said before we hung up.

The ride home was the longest drive of my life. I felt like the guy on one of those old prison movies on death row taking that long walk to the electric chair. I pulled up in my parking spot and sat there. My legs didn't want to move. I felt like I had cement blocks on my ankles. When I walked through the door and I saw Candy in the living room doing her work out to her work out video. She had a sweaty gloss on her. "Hey baby, how is your friend?" she asked. "Not so good" I said with a sad look on my face. She saw the expression on my face and turned off the work out video. I went into the kitchen, poured me a glass of hen and coke and sat at the kitchen table. "Isn't a little too early for that?" she asked me. "Not today, not today." I said to her. "I have something to tell you that may change everything you think about me. You may even hate me but I wouldn't blame you, I hate myself right now" I said to her looking down at my glass.

"Sammy, tell me what's wrong" Candy said to me. She sat down next to me and put her hand on my leg. "Candy, I'm not the perfect man you think I am." I said to her slowly. "Sammy, you don't have AIDS or some kind of disease do you? Kids I don't know about?" she asked quickly. "No, but I did make a mistake that shouldn't have happened. Candy, three months ago, when me and Toni went to the strip club, something happened." I confessed to her. "Sammy, what did you do?" she asked. "Well we were in the club drinking and having a good time. The next girl that came on stage we knew." I said to her. "Well who was it, an old girlfriend?" she asked me. "No, it was Tasha. She was working there." I told her. "So let me finish this for you. You slept with Tasha AGAIN! MY BEST FRIEND! The first time I couldn't be mad you for it, BUT THIS TIME, YOU BASTARD!" she said to me then hit me in the chest and started to walk up stairs. "That's not it," I told her standing up. "OH, WHAT ELSE, YOU TWO GOING TO BE A HAPPY COUPLE NOW? THAT BITCH, I KNEW SHE WAS A DIRTY BITCH, BUT YOU! I GAVE YOU MY LOVE; ALL OF ME; AND THIS IS HOW YOU REPAY ME? BITCH ASS NIGGA. WHAT? WHAT ELSE DO YOU HAVE TO TELL ME? HUH?" she screamed at me. "It wasn't just me" I said to her. "NASTY ASS BITCH! YOU TELLING ME THAT YOU AND YOUR SORRY ASS FRIEND RAN TRAIN ON MY BEST.....EX BEST FRIEND? ALL OF YOU ARE NASTY MUTHA FUCKAS!" she screamed as she ran to me and began hitting me uncontrolled manner. "BABY STOP! There's more," I said while covering up. She stopped hitting me and said "WHAT? WHAT ELSE YOU HAVE TO SAY!" she screamed again breathing hard. "Well, she says that she's pregnant and it's either mine or Toni's." I said to her. "MUTHA FUCKER" she screamed. She picked up the cord less phone and threw in at me but it didn't hit me because ducked. She ran upstairs crying. I ran after her. When I got up stairs she was packing the bag that she had brought with her. "Baby, I don't think you should drive anywhere," I said to her trying to hold her. "GET YOUR FUCKING HANDS OFF ME!" she said to me snatching away. I just stood there frozen while she packed her bag and put her clothes on. The whole time she was mumbling to herself. All of a sudden I fell to my knees and started crying. She stopped for a moment, look at me, but continued. She zipped up her bag and walked down stairs. As I fell from my knees to my face crying, I heard the front door slam and her car driving away very fast. For the first time in my life I was knocked down and didn't want get up. I laid there for the rest of the evening, feeling sorry for myself. Feeling sorry for all the bad things I had done to her. Just sorry.

I woke up the next morning feeling worse than I did yesterday. It was 9:30 am in the morning and I didn't want to get out of bed. I just wanted to lay there and do nothing, because that's how I felt, like nothing. I must have drunk the whole bottle of hen or at least I felt like it. I pulled the covers off me and I still had on the same clothes from yesterday. I went to bathroom feeling like a mess. I wanted to take a bath because I really needed to soak. As I put the stopper in the tub the phone rang. I didn't want to talk to anyone. I looked at the caller id. It was Candy calling. I answered it. "Hello" I said sadly. "Are you coming to church today?" she asked me. I could tell she was still upset by the sound of her voice. "Yes, if you want me to" I replied. "It isn't about what I want, are you coming or not?" she asked harshly. "I'm coming" I replied. Before I could say anything else, she hung up the phone. I pulled the stopper out of the tub so I could take a shower. I jumped in the shower feeling lost. "I wonder why she wants me to go to church with her?" I asked myself as the water ran down my face.

I got to the church about 10:35 am. As I looked at the front of the church I saw Candy standing with Tasha. "This can't be good," I said to myself. I wanted to keep on driving. But I can't lie, I was curious about what was going on. But you know the old saying curiosity killed the cat. I parked my car and walked up to them. Tasha didn't have on her usual short cut dress on. The dress she had on reached down pass her knee. When I finally got up to them, my head hang low. "Come on, let's go" Candy demanded. I felt like a child that had done something wrong and my mother was mad at them. The whole time in church I just sat there, listening with my head down. It felt like the preacher had talked to Candy because he went on and on about betrayal. We sat in the same positions as we did the last Sunday we all came to church. Candy leaned over to me and whispered "we're going to get something to eat afterwards and I want you to come also". I nodded and went back to listening.

After church we went to Popeye's. We sat there quietly eating our food. Candy broke the silence. "I wanted to get you two together so we can figure out what we're going to do. I'm still pissed, but I can't change what happened in the past. Sammy, maybe it's my fault" she said before I interrupted her. "Baby its" I said before she stopped me. "No, let me finish, and right now I'm not your baby. I don't know if I will ever be again. But Tasha, you're my best friend, but you have always been scandalous." Candy said. Tasha said nothing. "But I never thought you would be this scandalous. I love you like a sister, but now I know I can't trust you. Now as for this baby, Sammy, did you tell Toni?" she asked me. "Yes" I told her. "What does he think?" she asked. "He thinks that it isn't his or mine because of the type of strip club it was." I confessed. "And what type of club is that?" Tasha snapped. "The one where you can cut in the VIP room if you want for the right price" I said to her. "Well I never did all that, that wasn't my thing" Tasha answered me. "That's what your mouth say" I snapped at her. "You two quit it. Y'all weren't talking like this when you were fucking" Candy said to both of us. "Now Sammy, for right now, we are on standby. I will call you when I make a decision on if we are going to be together. I love you, which is why I'm talking to you right now. Have you cheated on me any other time?" Candy asked me. "No ba… no Candy, just this once, I've" I said before Candy cut me off. "Shut up. I believe you; just don't want to hear you right now. Ok, we can't find out who the baby's daddy is until you have it and our religion doesn't allow us to do the other thing and I wouldn't want to. That baby has the right to live. But I need a little distance from both of you right now. Let me know right now if you can't handle it" she said looking at both of us. "Yes" I answered. Tasha just nodded her head. "Now I don't know how long it's going to be, I'm going to pray to God about it. It maybe three months, it could be three days, it could be forever. Sammy, if we were meant to be, we will. Tasha, we have known each other for a while. That's why I haven't jumped up and whooped your ass, plus you're pregnant. I knew something was wrong, I knew it." Candy said starting to cry. I tried to comfort her. She snatched away for me and stood up. "Let's go." she said to us. We walked outside. "Don't let me hear about you two fucking around. Sammy come here." she said walking away. "Candy, I'm sorry" Tasha said crying. Candy just kept on walking and I followed. When we got to her car she turned around and slapped me. I took it and looked away. When I did I saw Tasha walk to her car and drive off. "You have made me the happiest women and the saddest women all in the same day. But I'm sorry for putting my hands on you." she said to me. I looked at her like she was crazy. "How was she going to say that right after she just slapped me?" I thought to myself. "Sammy, I love you, I love you. You hurt me, but I blame you and myself at the same time. If I didn't let my past hold me back from you, this might not have happened. Plus you two have history. Maybe we shouldn't have gotten together in the first place. I don't mean to leave you hanging like this. And if you can't wait on me, I understand, but I need to think about this." Candy said holding my face where she slapped me. "Candy, I'll wait as long as you need me to. I should have waited before. I was the fool. But I won't be that fool again. You take your time, I'll be waiting," I said looking into her eyes. We both had hurt in our eyes. I never cried so much in front of a female. Not even my mother. It hurt to be like this. I wish we could have stayed happy like before. She gave me a soft kiss on the lips. This kiss was a very painful kiss because I didn't know if it would be the last kiss I will receive from her. She is the love of my life. I just hoped she would come back to me.

CHAPTER SEVEN
All that and I didn't even get a nut

Time had passed pretty quickly after that Sunday with Candy, three months to be exact. I had not talk to her much since that horrible day. She would call and see how I was doing, but nothing more. I didn't want to bring up the fact of when we will get back together, because she never mentioned it. She always added that she was alone and not seeing anyone. I hadn't met up with any females myself. I just go to work and straight home. Toni would come over like always. Nothing had changed between him and me. He was really enjoying the mailroom job but always complained about the pay. "You're going to get paid dawg, it's just going to take a minute" I would tell him. But I could tell he was getting impatient.

Surprisingly Tasha hadn't call me much either. She would tell me about her doctors' appointments and how the baby was kicking her butt. But as for her trying to become more to me, no mention of it. So everything was normal but lonely for me at this time in my life. I wanted Candy back but I had no control over that situation. I just have to be patient and be here when she wants me. But how long do I wait? How long will I wait?

It had been a long time since I had taken a day off in the middle of the week, but I had some stuff to take care of. That morning I went to the doctor's office for my six month checkup. All was well with me, though the doctor told me I could work on my cholesterol. After that I decided to play around with my car. I had backed it up into my car spot with the hood up. I was looking at my engine wondering how I could make it run better when my cell phone began to ring. My phone was on my passenger seat so I went to the passenger side of the car, reached in through the window and picked it up. It was a number I didn't recognize.

"Hello" I said speaking into the phone. "Hello, can I speak to Sammy?" a women with a sweet voice asked. "This is Sammy right here" I answered. "You may not remember me, but a couple of months ago you gave me a ride home and" she said before I interrupted her. "TONIA!" I said with excitement in my voice. "Yeah, I'm surprised that you remembered me. It's been a long time," she said with surprise. "Well, it's kind of hard to forget a pretty lady like yourself. What's been going on with you?" I asked. "Well I just moved into my new apartment and I found your number in a stack of papers so I decided to call you. I'm not disturbing you, am I?" she asked me. "Knaw, just playing around with my car. I took the day off." I told her. "Oh a working man. I like that. Better than these guys I have been dealing with all these years" she said with disappointment in her voice. "Oh, I'm sorry about that. My ol' lady and me are going through some things. I got caught up in some mess and now I'm paying for it" I confessed to her. "Paying for it how?" she asked. "Well we are on time out until she is ready" I told her. "And how long has this time out lasted?" she asked. "It's been about three months now" I said to her. "THREE MONTHS! That seems like more than time out. You're a good man for waiting this long" she told me. "I'm trying to do right by her. I really do love her but enough about that. How does it feel not to live at home anymore?" I asked her changing the subject. "I love it. I finally feel like an adult. I got a nice little job, nice little car. I just wish I had a good man. But out here in LA, it's easier said than done" she told me. "Hey, that's what Easy E said" I told her with a laugh. "Boy you so silly. What you got planned this evening?" she asked me. "Nothing, sit around the house and get ready for work tomorrow. Why what's up?" I asked her. "Nothing, I just feel like cooking but I don't want to cook just for myself. I'm still used to cooking for other people" she said to me. "Yeah, what do you feel like cooking?" I asked her. "Some short ribs, cornbread, and corn, something like that" she said. "Damn girl, you making my mouth water. How you learn to cook like that?" I asked her. "My family is from Alabama. My mom taught me everything I need to know to catch a man with food" she told me with a laugh. "Cooking like that, you are damn right" I told her. "Well if you're not doing anything, why don't you come by?" she said to me. "It sounds tempting, but I don't know. I'm still going through this stuff with my girl. I don't feel right going to another woman's house" I confessed to her. "It's only to eat, it ain't even all that. Come on, I want you to see my new place anyway, please?" she asked me. I thought about it. "I am hungry" I thought to myself. "Alright" I said. She gave me the directions to her place and hung up. I closed all the doors on my car, set the alarm and headed for the house. I looked out to the road and I saw that same black truck again which was strange, because it had been months since I last saw it. "What is going on?" I asked myself as I went into the house.

It was five o'clock in the evening. I was getting ready to go over to Tonia's. I would be telling a lie if I said I didn't think about hitting that. But like I told her, I'm trying to make this thing work with Candy. As I was buttoning up my black dress shirt the phone rang. I looked at the caller id and it was Candy. I pick up the phone and said "hey Candy, what's up?" "Nothing much, I just thought about you and I decided to call. What are you doing?" she asked me. "I'm about to go get something to eat. Why? What's going on?" I asked her. "Nothing, I just wanted to come by and hang out for a little bit. But if you're busy I'll check with you later" she said to me. "Damn, ain't this a bitch." I thought to myself. I knew that this might be the day that I have been waiting for since we had parted. But at the same time, I told Tonia that I was coming over and she has cooked all this food. "What time are you thinking you will be over her?" I asked her. "Right now if that's cool with you?" she stated. "Fuck." I thought. "Cool, come on over." I said to her. "Alright, see you in a few, bye" she said before hanging up the phone. "Ok, what do I do now?" I asked myself. I dialed Tonia's number. "Hello" she answered. "Hey pretty lady. What are you doing?" I asked her. "I'm getting everything ready to cook as we speak" she replied. "Good" I thought to myself. "Hey Tonia, I'm sorry, but some things came up at the last minute. I'm not going to be able to come by. I'm sorry." I told her. "Oh, what happened?" she asked. I had to think fast. "My friend got stranded on the highway and I have to go get him" I told her. "Oh, yeah you better go. LA highways are not the place to be standing around. One of these fools might run him over, just because" she replied. "Thank you for being so understanding, I'll pay you back, I promise" I told her. "Yeah, you owe me dinner, so get ready to pay up. Just call me when you get back to the house so I know you're safe" Tonia requested. "Alright and thanks again. Bye-bye" I said before hanging up.

About fifteen minutes later, my doorbell rang. I looked in the mirror one more time to make sure I was looking my best and then opened the door. I opened it up a crack and saw Candy standing there with a busted grey jogging suit on. "May I help you little girl?" I asked her. "Quit playing and let me in silly ass boy," she said with a smile on her face. She came in and sat on the couch. "Don't you look all good? I didn't stop you from going somewhere special, did I?" she asked me. "Knaw, just to this soul food place. What's going on with you? I see you look all relaxed" I said to her. I needed to get out of my place. One of my roommates and her boyfriend are having a disagreement. And I don't want to hear all that." she said to me. "Well I'm glad you chose to come over. I miss you Candy. I miss you a lot" I said to her sadly. "I miss you too. What you got to eat in here?" she said as she popped to her feet fast. "Um, you can check out the ice box, I'm going to get changed" I told her. I ran upstairs and took off the clothes I had on and put on a tank top and some basketball shorts. As I was walking down stairs I could smell microwave pizza cooking. "How can I go from having a full course country meal to microwave pizza?" I asked myself.

When I walked into the kitchen Candy was watching the pizza spin around and round in the microwave. I walked up behind her and wrapped my arms around her. "Boy, what you think you are doing?" she asked me. "Nothing" I replied. She didn't jerk away from me she just continued to watch the pizza. I tried to kiss her neck then she told me "you need to stop" and then broke out of my arms. She took the pizza out of the microwave. I thought to myself, "do something", so when she walked past me trying to go back into the living room I grabbed the pizza out of her hand and ran to the living room. "Boy, quit playing. I'm too hungry to chase you around" she said as she ran after me. I danced around the living room avoiding her. Then I ran back into the kitchen and put the pizza behind my back. "Give me my pizza fool," she said to me. "Give me a kiss and I'll give you the pizza" I said to her. She leaned back as she looked at me. "Give me the pizza Sammy, NOW!" she said. "Or what" I asked her.

She stood there with her hands on her hips. "Or what?" she said before grabbing my balls with her hand. "Ouch, hey girl, that shit hurts" I said to her. "Well give me the pizza, I ain't playing" she said with a grin. "I don't know, I think I like it." I said with a smile on my face. As she held me in her hands my dick began to stiffen. She looked down at it then looked at me in the face. I put the pizza down on the counter and began to kiss her passionately. She began kissing me back, rubbing my balls up and down. Then she snatched away from me. "No, we have to stop, we have to stop." she said to me. "No we don't" I said to her grabbing her close to me. "We can do whatever we want" I said before kissing her again.

As before, she kissed me back with the same passion. I took my right hand a put it down in her pants. I could feel the heat from her pussy on my fingertips. I took my middle finger and rubbed it on her sweet spot. She was nice and moist. I guess that all this was too much for her so she backed up and took my hand out of her pants. "Sammy, I want you and I want this, really I do. But this is not right for me right now. I going to leave" she said to me heading to the door. "Candy wait. If you're not ready, I'm not ready, but you don't have to leave. Stay. I will show you that it's not all about that. Stay, please" I pleaded to her. She stopped and turned around. "Ok Sammy because I really don't want to leave. I want to be here with you" she said to me with a tear in her eye. "And I want you to be here with me. Come and sit down. We'll watch Fighting Temptations together" I said with a smile on my face. She smiled and said to me "I would like that. I would like that a lot. But what about after that?" she asked me. "If you don't want to go back to your spot, you can sleep in my bed and I'll sleep down here on the couch" I told her. "I'm not going to put you out your bed. I'll sleep on the couch" she said to me. "Knaw, you know what, lets both sleep in the bed. You just stay on your side of the bed and don't try to get all freaky with me" I said to her with a laugh. "Boy you better stay on YOUR side. You're the horn ball here" she said to me joking. "Hey you shouldn't have grabbed the balls. I'm sensitive" I said to her. For the rest of the night we talked and watched the movie. It was just like old times. I really did miss her. But I still felt like I was missing out on something with Tonia.

Candy went to bed after watching the movie. I stayed down stairs getting ready for a presentation I had the next day. When 10:30 came around the phone rang. It was Tonia. "Hello" I said answering the phone. "What happened? You was supposed to call me when you got back home" she said to me with a tone in her voice. "I'm so sorry, when I got back, I had to work on this presentation for work" I said to her. "Presentation? Professional man. I love professional men, they make my pussy wet?" she said to me with a sexy voice. I thought to myself "did I just hear, what I thought I heard?" "Excuse me?" I asked Tonia. "Professional men make my pussy wet" she repeated. "Well I do try. So is it wet right now?" I asked her. "Oh yes, very wet, dripping wet, oozing wet" she said to me. "Damn girl, that sounds so edible. How do you know all that?" I asked. "Well, I got my hand on it right now. My fingers are just dripping right now. Oh, sorry about that" she said to me sounding like she was pleasuring herself. "Lucky fingers. Why don't you rub your index finger on your clit, close your eyes and imagine that it's my tongue licking it up and down" I said to her. "Ok, oh, aahhh, oooohhhhh, lick it baby" she said to me moaning. "You like that, huh, you like that tongue on your tasty clit?" I asked her. "Yes, ooohhhh, it feel ssssooo good" she replied. "Yeah, well doing it faster girl, faster. That shit taste so good. Your pussy is so sweet" I said to her. "Oh Sammy, lick it baby. Oh it feels so good, I wish you was here" she said to me. "Don't worry about that, just think about my tongue licking you" I said to her. "Yes big daddy" she said. "Big daddy? Ok" I said to myself laughing. "Yeah, let big daddy lick you down" I told her. "Yes big daddy, yes big daddy. You're the shit big daddy" she said to me moaning.

I wanted to laugh so badly, but at the same time, my dick was so fucking hard. Candy was upstairs but she was not going to do anything with me. So I went to the bathroom and got some tissue while she was still moaning. Pulled out my dick and started stroking it back and forth. "Oh yeah girl, now do you have one of those things?" I asked her. "What things? Dill Doe?" she asked. "Yeah one of those" I said to her. "Yeah, it's right here" she replied. "Ok, take it in your hand and slide it in you pussy really slow" I said to her. "Oooohhhhhh, God, mmm" I heard her say. "Sound like it's been a while" I said to her. "Yes. It's so tight" she whispered to me. "Yeah I can feel it" I said to her with my hand wrapped tightly around my dick. "What are you doing over there?" she asked with a whisper. "I got my dick in my hand acting like that tight, wet, juicy pussy is wrapped around me right now" I told her. "Okay, that's sounds fun" she replied. "Ok, now slide it in deep as you can" I told her. "Oooohhhhh, ooooohhhhh, mmm" I heard her moan. When she did that I slid my hand down the shaft of my dick like I was in her pussy. "Now bring it out slow all the way to the tip and then back in slow and deep" I said to her while stroking my dick the way I just describe to her. "Oh yeah, I like it like that big daddy" she said to me. "I like it like that too. Just keep on doing it like that. Nice and slow, nice and deep" I told her. "Oh God, it feels so good" she moaned. "Yeah, now speed it up a little, out and in, out and in" I said to her. "Oh yes big daddy, put it on me" she said. "Now faster, and faster, oh shit" I said while stroking my dick back and forward. "Oh yes, is feels so good, oh baby I'm about to cum, big daddy" she moaned. "Oh yeah? Get yours. I'm about to cum too" I said to her moaning. "OH YES, OH YES BIG DADDY!" she screamed. That made me want to cum too, then out oh now where, "SAMMY! WHAT ARE

YOU DOING DOWN THERE?" Candy yelled from the bedroom. "UM, NOTHING, JUST FINISHING UP!" I yelled covering up the phone. I could still hear Tonia going off in the background moaning. I whispered into the phone "I got to go, call you tomorrow" Tonia replied out of breath "ok big daddy, good night" and then hung up the phone. I started putting everything away, cut off the TV and headed up stairs. "All that, and I didn't even get a nut" I said to myself before pulling the covers over me as I lay in the bed.

CHAPTER EIGHT
You live and you learn

Candy and I were almost back to normal. It had been a month since she came to my house. Now she was coming to the house on a daily occasion and that was a good thing. Today Toni and me were on our way to the pool hall to drink a couple of beers and play a little pool. It had been a while since we hung out other than work.

When we got to the pool hall it was rather empty. "Damn cuz, I miss chilling with you. The mail room got me so tired; all I want to do when I get off is smoke something and go to bed. I don't know how you do this hard working shit all this time" Toni said while taking aim at the white pool ball on the table. "Well, hard work is all I know. Back in the Miss, I used to hail hay in the summer, go to school, and play sports" I replied. "See that was my problem. I wanted to be in the streets, slanging, banging, sometimes I wish my pops had stayed. Maybe my life would be better" Toni confessed to me. "Knaw, it could have been worse. How was it when he was there?" I asked Toni. "It was good until I was like five. My mom and dad would argue all the time. I think about money. She wanted more and he couldn't supply. So he got fed up and bounced. I don't blame him but he forgot about me. Now he got his new family. I don't even see him that much. And when I do see him, he always tells me to be better than what I am. Don't sell drugs, be a man. But hell, I had to teach myself how to be a man because he was raising somebody else's kids. So I was like fuck it cuz. Rack 'em" Toni said to me after knocking the eight ball into the right top corner of the pool table. "Nigga you think you tight" I said with a laugh. "Man, I'm a mutha fucking professional on this pool shit. I should be on TV with that Chinese lady. The Black Widow" he said with a laughing.

The laughing didn't last long. Three guys came into the pool hall looking and pointing in Toni's direction. "Who the fuck is that Toni" I asked him. "That's Big Rob and his brother's. That's the guys I used to slang for" Toni replied. The three guys walked over to the table. "TONI! What's going on man? Long time, no see" Big Rob said to Toni. "What's going on Big Rob" Toni replied with a serious look on his face. "This is my man" Toni said before one of Big Rob's brothers interrupted him. "Sammy, what's going on? I'm Craig and this is my little brother James" Craig said to me. "Say man, how the hell you know me, dawg?" I asked him with a strong tone. "Calm down cuz. I used to see you run for USC. You was a fast mutha fucka. Too bad you never tried out for the Olympics. Oh yeah, you did, then your bitch ass choked up and got SMOKED!" Craig said with a big smile on his face. "What the fuck you say to me BITCH?" I said to him starting to walk in his direction. Toni put his arm in front of me and shook his head. "Yeah bitch, do like the other bitch and stay where you are at" James said to me lifting up his shirt showing the gun he had in his pants waist band. "Y'all calm down" Big Rob said. "That's no way to talk to a celebrity. He brought many medals to USC and I thank you for that. We just wanted to speak to Toni about something" Big Rob said while looking at Toni. "Well, he doesn't have anything to say, plus we are in the middle of a game" I said to Big Rob. "I see that, I just wanted to congratulate Toni on his new job. It's good that he stopped fucking with the street life. Good on you. But when that little change that you are making isn't good enough for you, hit me up. You can have your old job back" Big Rob said to Toni. "Knaw cuz, I'm cool" Toni replied. "Ok, well you fella's enjoy your game" Big Rob said before heading towards the door. "See you later, bitch" Craig said looking in my direction.

After they left we decided that it was time to go. As we drove down the road, we decided to take a drive down Century. That's where all of the hoe's walked the street. I was always intrigued by the street life, but could get into it myself. I guess it was the way I was raised. "What the fuck was that all about Toni?" I asked. "They want me to work for them again. They keep fucking with me about it" Toni replied. "That shit ain't for you dawg" I told him. "I know cuz, I know. BUT WHAT THE FUCK!" Toni said to me. "What dawg?" I asked him. "Nigga, you think your tough than a mutha. What were you going to do to Big Rob and his brother's?" Toni asked me laughing. "Man, I was going to put them thangs on them, boy" I said laughing. "Your ass was going to get us shot. Your ass needs to go back to the country with that fighting shit. Don't nobody fight in Cali. They shoot first homie" Toni said to me. "It's all good, they may have got me in the rush, but the first cat was going to feel me, fo reel" I said holding up my right fist. "Yeah, yeah. But look at that bitch right there" Toni said pointing out the window at one of the prostitutes on the road. "She does have a phat booty. But I can't bring myself to pick up on of them hoes. Just my luck, I'll be on one of those America Undercover shows" I said laughing. "Knaw cuz, I picked up one the other day. She gave me some bomb head. It was only twenty-dollars" Toni said. "What made you pick her up?" I asked him. "I was on my way home from work and I was tired, but not ready to go home. So I took a ride up here. I saw her and thought about it. Then I didn't want to because it was broad daylight but I said fuck it. Pulled over, asked her if she needed a ride. She took me to a back street, did her thing and I dropped her off where I found her" Toni told me like he was giving me some kind some hoe pick up directions. "So she bopped you real good huh?" I asked him. "Yep, I went home, played PlayStation, and knocked the fuck out, cuz" he replied. We both laughed and finally made it to his house. "Aright, cuz. See you at work tomorrow" Toni said to me getting out my car. "Say dawg, the car is starting to look right" I said looking at how much effort he had put into his car trying to restore it. It was a 1988 white Chevy Caprice. "You might be up there with Ced one day." I said to him smiling. "Fuck that nigga cuz, my car is better than his now." Toni replied. "Alright then playa, stay up" I replied to him before driving off.

After dropping off Toni I decided to take one more swing through Century. I could have used the 210 highway to get to the 405, but I wanted to take one more good look at some scattered ass before I went home. As I was driving down century my cell phone rang. I answered it "hello". "Hey boy, it's Tonia." "Hey, how are you doing sexy?" I asked her with excitement. I hadn't talked to her since the phone sex we had. "Nothing much, I have been kind of busy working and stuff. I just got off and you popped in my mind. What are you doing?" she asked me. "I'm driving down Century headed to the 405. I just dropped my dawg off, now I'm heading home" I told her. "Toni?" she asked. "Yeah" I replied. "Well since you're by my apartment, why don't you stop by?" she asked me. After that conversation with Toni about that good head and the flashback of the phone sex we had, I was ready to get me a little. "Sure, where you stay?" I asked. "Where are you?" she asked. "I'm at the light by the Great western forum." I told her. Well make a right there and the third light after that, make a left and I will be outside" she replied. "Cool, I'm on my way." I said to her.

I followed her directions and she was standing outside with her arms crossed like she was cold. She had on some pink Baby Phat daisy dukes, with a pink shirt to match. I parked my car and walked up to her. She gave me a big hug and leaned back. "Have you been working out?" she asked as she rubbed her hands up and down my arms. "I do a little something. You are really wearing those clothes, damn you fucking with a nigga" I said to her looking at her body. "That was the whole point. Let's go in the house" she said pulling me towards the apartment.

She lived on the second floor of this old looking, dark apartment building. You could see kid toys all over the place. In the stairway it smelled like piss as we walked up. I didn't picture her living in a place like this but I guess some people will do anything to get out of a bad situation.

When we got up to her apartment, it was completely different from the outside. Nice clean, bright colors, it had a good vibe about it. She had a tan love seat and coffee table and a 27 inch TV sitting on a desk in the living room. The kitchen was really big. As I sat on the couch, she turned off the lights so the light from the TV was the only light in the room. She sat right under me, wrapping her arms around me and throwing her right leg on my lap. When I focused on the TV there was a black porno playing. "Girl, you don't fuck around do you?" I asked her while rubbing on her leg. "I'm the kind of woman that knows what I want and I go after it. I don't play games. Games are for children and I'm not a child. I'm a full, grown woman" she said to me standing up.

When she stood up, she rubbed her hands all over her body. "Don't I look like a full grown woman to you, Sammy" she asked me. "Hell yeah, a full grown woman" I replied to her. She did a little dance, turned around and slow swung her ass in my face. I sat there with my hands on my lap watching her. "Don't be afraid, go ahead and touch it. I know you want to" she said to me looking over her right shoulder. I took my right hand and slowly rubbed her right butt cheek. It was so soft and smooth. I could feel my dick get stiff in my pants. "Damn baby girl, your ass is off the chains" I said to her looking into her eyes. "I'm glad that you like it" she said before walking away then turning around. I put my hand back on my lap, covering my dick. I didn't want her to see my dick getting hard. She swung her hips three more times and then walked out of the living room into another room. "Sammy, could you come here for a minute?" she asked me from the other room. I jumped up off the couch and about near ran in the other room.

I entered the room, and it was completely lit by candlelight. She had a nice three-piece bedroom set, with a pink comforter and pink and white fluffy pillows. The main dresser had a big mirror in it. It candles reflected off of it nicely. Tonia was in the bathroom that was on the other side of this room. "Have a seat on the bed" she told me. I sat on the bed and leaned back on my elbows. She was in the bathroom for about ten minutes then she came out wear some kind of fishnet outfit with nothing on under it. It fit her body like a glove. She walked over to me and spread my legs apart. She got on her knees in between my legs and started to undo my pants. She pulled down my pants with a little assistance from me and then she pulled my dick out of my boxers. She held it in her hand and said to me "very nice. Better than I imagined. Something about you south boys" "Why thank you" I replied to her. She smiled and said "see Sammy, I know a good man when I see him and I think you are a good man. Good job, good attitude, good size dick, I need a good man like you with me. I know you got a woman, but she is not treating you the way I can. I would never make you wait on me for nothing. I would treat you like you deserve to be treated. Like a king."

After she said that, she put my dick in her mouth and began sucking it. It was so warm and she really knew how to get it all wet without it looking disgusting or nasty. She used two hands and a lot of spit, just the way I like it. It was so good that I was about to bust only after a couple of seconds. Then right when I was there she took my dick out of her mouth and began talking again. "See, you would get this every day, all day, any time that you wanted or needed it. If you was my man, but since you're not." After she said that she put my dick back in my boxers and stood up.

I laid on the bed with a confused look on my face. Then I thought to myself "OH HELL KNAW!" I stood up, kicked of my pants, slid off my boxers, picked her up and laid her on the bed. She began to laugh. I climbed up to her chest and straddled her with my legs. I ripped open the fish net outfit where her breast was, took her breasts in my hands and wrapped my dick with them. She bit her bottom lip like this was really turning her on. I started moving my dick back and forward in her breast. Her breasts were so soft and felt so good wrapped around me. I never titty fucked a women before. I pump my dick in and out, in and out. She softly rubbed my thighs as I did this. I start to go faster and faster until it was time to climax. I thought about if I should tell her or not. But by the time I was going to tell her the first explosion of cum shot out and hit her on her bottom lip, another shot out, and then she grabbed my dick and put it in her mouth. I felt like I was a milkshake and she was trying to suck the last drop out of me. The sensation was overwhelming. It felt like a river flowing through me and into her. I never felt a feeling like this in my life. The sensation became so intense that I had to take my dick out of her mouth and lay down.

I felt drained, but yet my dick was still hard. I laid beside her as she used her fingers to rub the rest of the cum she didn't swallow on her chest. The she rolled over to the side of the bed and open up the top dresser drawer beside the bed. She pulled out a magnum condom and her dildo. "Knaw baby boy, you're not done yet" she said to me while she put the condom on my dick. She climbed on my dick backwards with her ass facing me. Her ass looked outstanding on my dick like that. She slid my dick into her pussy. It was dripping wet; she must have really been turned on. She started riding my dick hard and fast like a wild woman. The shit was crazy! I didn't know how to feel, scared or happy.

Then she looked over her shoulder and asked "you like this? You like it big daddy?" I said to her in a plain voice "yes" because my dick was numb and could hardly feel anything. Then she handed me the dildo and said "here, put this in my ass". I look at her with a bewildered look on my face and said "do what?" "Put this up my ass" she said as she bounced up and down on my dick like a pogo stick. "Alright" I said as I took it in my hands. It was already lubed up with something. So I started to stick it in slowly. She stopped riding me. I felt her booty cheeks tighten. "Yeah, just like that. Nice and slow" she said moaning. When I got it all the way in, she slowly started riding my again. About this time, the feeling in my dick had come back. So I was feeling pretty good but weird at the same time. Then she said to me "fuck me doggie style". "Alright" I replied to her. She got off me with the dildo still stuck in her ass and bent over on the bed. When she leaned over on the bed the dildo popped out like a plastic pop gun bullet. I got behind her and stuck my dick in her pussy then put the dildo back in her ass. I was going at a slow pace when she yelled at me "FUCK ME HARD!" So I said to myself "fuck it", and started pounding her as hard as I could. Her ass was smacking hard on my thighs and the dildo sticking me in my stomach with every thrust.

The whole time I wasn't concentrating on getting a nut, I kept looking at the dildo in her ass think how that should hurt. Then she said to me "FUCK ME IN THE ASS!" "What you say?" I asked her. "FUCK ME IN THE ASS WITH YOUR BIG DICK, BIG DADDY" she screamed as I was stroking her as fast as I could. "Alright" I repeated once again. I took the dildo out and slid my dick in. I had never done this before, but I was always curious about it. It wasn't like though it would be. The hole was extra tight but not as wet as a pussy. Me not knowing any better, I started fucking her ass like it in was her pussy. But she liked that shit. "YES! FUCK MY ASS, FUCK THE SHIT OUT OF MY ASS!" she screamed. And I did. "PULL MY HAIR, SMACK MY ASS!" she screamed. And I did. I was laughing and screamed, "YEAH, TAKE THIS SHIT!" It was more entertaining than a turn on. "YES! YES! IM CUMMING!" she screamed. "Cumming?" I thought to myself. She collapsed to the bed so I stopped fucking her and just stood there in disbelief. "DAMN! That was better than I imagined" she said out of breath. "Ooo kkkkkk, I glad you enjoyed it" I said to her then smacking her on her ass. I walked towards the bathroom to wash up. "Where are you going?" she asked me still out of breath. "To wash up" I replied to her. "Oh, ok" she replied and just laid there. I went into the bathroom and wiped my dick with a face towel, soap and water.

When I came back out, Tonia was sleep on the bed. I put on my clothes and picked her up. I moved back the comforter at the head of the bed, laid her down and covered her up. When I walked out the house, I made sure I locked the door, because this is not the place to leave your door unlocked. I walked to my car thinking "that was the wildest shit that has ever happened to me. Wait until I tell Toni this shit." At a time like this, I should have been very happy, but I wasn't. It seemed like it was just something to do. She was someone to help me jack my dick off. Sex just has not felt the same to me since I made love to Candy. Before I didn't know that there was a difference between having sex and making love, but now I know. It's fucked up how I learn truth about things after I fuck up and do the wrong thing. I guess that is what life is all about. You live and you learn from different experiences.

CHAPTER NINE
This could mess up things for all of us

Well it was about that time for Tasha to have the baby. I had a certain vibe that the baby wasn't mine. Maybe it was wishful thinking, but that is how I felt. It was the fourth of July and we were having a bar-b-que at the beach. This had been a tradition of me and Toni for years. But this year we had a lot more people than normal. It was going to be me, Toni, Candy, Ced, Tammy, Tammy's friend Tametra and her boyfriend, Tammy's parents and her little brother.

Now I felt a little uncomfortable with Tametra coming but Tammy promised me she wouldn't trip, plus her old man would be there to calm that down. See Tametra was one of those women that just had to make a good time into a bad time. I got to the beach pretty early to secure a spot because everyone and their momma would be out there. It was a nice California morning. The sun was out; the sky is clear and blue, very nice. I liked the peace of being by myself at the beach. I could think clearly without any outside interference. Candy was supposed to come out and chill with me, but she was still at my crib sleeping. Sometimes I swear that she was pregnant the way that she slept. Me and her had been chilling a lot lately, like before all the drama happened. I knew that she really cares for me. I put her through a lot and she is still here with me. I had not done anything wrong since that night with Tonia. I was beginning to realize that all the running around, playing around on Candy was not worth it. I have a great woman with me who can please my mind, body, and soul. Something all those other women could not do. Every one of them was missing something, but she has it all.

It was about 12:00 pm when everyone started coming. "Sorry I'm late cuz, I couldn't wake up for some reason" Toni said to me giving me dap. "It's all good dawg, it wasn't like I was expecting you to get up" I said to him with a big smile on my face. "Fuck all that cuz. Here's the stuff you wanted me to bring" Toni replied. I asked him to bring the plates, plastic spoons, folks, and knives. "I also brought the drank cuz. We are going to get fucked up. Plus I got the weed for me" Toni said while holding up the bag of green sticky. "Well you know this is a public beach, don't get caught because I don't know you when you do" I said to him while turning my back to him. "See, you a bitch ass dude" Toni said to me laughing. "It's only funny because you're telling the truth, hoe ass nigga" "Yep, I'll be that" I replied to him.

About that time I saw Candy walking up holding a lot of bags. I ran up to her. "Here baby, let me help you with those" I said to her grabbing the bags. She had the bags of meat I had seasoned the night before, some potato salad she had made, and a familiar looking purse bag. "Candy, this your bag?" I asked while holding up the purse. "That is Tasha's bag. She is getting out of the car right now. She shouldn't be carrying nothing being nine months pregnant and all" Candy replied to me. I didn't expect Tasha to come. Now it's really going to be awkward. "Since she might be part of the family, she might as well get used to hanging around the rest of the folks we know" Candy said to me. "True, true" I replied not really wanting to hear it. When we got back to the table I looked at Toni and shook my head. "What cuz?" he asked me. Right when he said that, Tasha came walking up, big stomach and all. "Hell knaw cuz. What the fuck is this?" Toni yelled out. I gave him a look like "what the fuck". Candy said to Toni "Don't do that, because you wasn't saying that a couple months ago. Don't act like that now." Toni looked at me, but I just put my head down and started taking the stuff out the bags. "Hey y'all" Tasha said walking up to the table. "Hey Tasha" Toni and Me replied in a low voice. "I thought y'all would have something cooked, a bitch is hungry," Tasha said while rubbing her stomach. "Knaw we don't have nothing for your swollen, hungry ass" Toni said to her. "Hey, stop that Toni" Candy said to Toni. "I was just joking, you know I can talk to my baby momma like that" Toni said to Candy with a laugh. "Fuck you nigga, fuck you" Tasha said to

Toni. "You already did, and you llllooovvvveeeedddd it" Toni said to her while rubbing her stomach. I didn't want to laugh or even smile because I could feel Candy's eyes burning on the back of my head.

As that was going on, I could see Ced, Tammy, Mr. and Mrs. Jones, J.R., Tametra and her boyfriend walking up. "What's going on dawg?" I said to Ced giving him a hand slap and a hung. "Nothing much man. Ready to get my grub on. Did y'all spark the grille yet?" Ced said to me. "Just now, it should be ready to cook in about ten minutes or so." I replied to him. "Hey Mrs. Jones" I said to her before giving her and tight hug. "Watch out now boy. That's a married woman you got there" Mr. Jones said to me before sitting down on the concrete bench. "Sorry Mr. Jones, I just could resist a beautiful woman like this" I said with a smile on my face. "Shut up little boy, I would break you" Mrs. Jones replied. "OOOOHHHHHH!" everyone yelled, including Mr. Jones. "You better leave my momma a lone" Tammy said to me hitting me in the back of my head. "Hey now girl, watch the hair" I replied to her. "Now Tammy, you don't see me smacking Ced around" Candy said coming to my defense. "HEY GIRL! Long time, no see," Tammy said to Candy before giving her a hug. "How have you been?" Tammy asked Candy. "I'm doing well, hey this is Tasha" Candy said to Tammy. "Hi" Tammy said in a monotone voice. "Hi" Tasha replied. "Tasha, this is my mom and dad Mr. And Mrs. Jones, my little brother J.R., and my fiancé' Ced." Tammy said introducing everyone to her. "Hi everyone" Tasha replied. "So, how many months are you?" Mrs. Jones asked Tasha. "Nine months, ma'am" Tasha replied. "Is the father coming today?" Mrs. Jones asked. Everyone got quiet. "Um, no, he will not be attending ma'am" Tasha replied with a slight smile. "Come on over here" Mr. Jones said while pulling Mrs. Jones to sit down by him. Apparently Tammy didn't give Mrs. Jones the memo on what happened. It was quiet for a minute, until Toni turned on the boom box with old school music playing. "Who got the bones?" Ced yelled out. "I got them mutha fuckers cuz. I'm going to show y'all how we do in Cali, fo real." Toni said taking out the dominos.

It was about 2 o'clock when all the ribs, chicken, and pork chops were done. So we had potato salad, greens, baked beans and cheesecake. The guys ate at one table and the females at the other. Everyone was having a good time until Jazmin and Tonia walked up the sidewalk. I have to admit, they were looking good ass hell. Jazmin had on some biker shorts and a sports bra-looking thing and Tonia had on some Apple Bottom daisy dukes and Apple Bottom baby shirt. Their bodies were on point. The females smirked and the males sat quiet and looked. Toni and I looked at each other like "oh shit". They had some nerve because they walked right up to where Toni and me were. "Hey Sammy, what's going on? Look like a good ass BBQ going on" Tonia said to me. "Yeah, we're trying to do a little something out here. What brings y'all to the beach," I said with a shaky voice. "My cousin is having a cook out on the other side" Jazmin replied. "Oh, that's straight" I replied to her. Out of the corner of my eye I could see Candy getting up and heading in our direction. "Uh oh cuz" Toni whispered to me. "Hey baby, this is Jazmin and Tonia," I said to her quickly grabbing her and sitting her on my lap. "Nice to meet you, I'm Candy" Candy said to them. "How you doing girl? Nice to meet you also" Jazmin said. Tonia just rolled her eyes. "Anyway, we just wanted to speak, you all enjoy your meal. Come on Jazmin" Tonia said before walking off. "Sammy. Who was that?" Candy asked me. "Candy, that's a bitch I used to fuck with back in the days and the one that had attitude was her friend that Sammy dissed when she wanted to fuck" Toni told Candy. "Oh, ok" she replied before standing up and going back over to the rest of the females. "Thanks dawg" I said to Toni, giving him dap. "You fucked that bitch?" Ced asked me. "Yeah and she's a freak too. She had me put dildos up her ass, fuck her in the ass, everything." I replied to him. "What you say there boy?" Mr. Jones asked. He like hearing the young guys tell our freaky sex stories. It made him feel like he was doing it he told us once. "Yeah, and the dome was off the chains. She deep throat my shit so deep, I could feel the back of her head." I said to them.

All the guys started laughing really loud. The females looked at us with squinted eyes. They knew we were talking about something we were not supposed to talk about. But it was all in fun. "So, what's up with that Tasha girl?" Mr. Jones asked. "Well that's a messed up situation. She says the baby could be me or Toni's baby, but the way she freaked us down, who knows." I replied to him. "Yeah that freak was off the meter cuz," Toni said to Ced. "She backed that ass up, sucked a nigga down like no other." "Sammy, didn't you beat her down while you was in college?" Ced asked me. "Yeah once, but it wasn't like that night me and Toni ran up in. WHOA BOY!" I said with a laugh. "But I don't like talking about it. I almost lost my women over that shit. I still can't understand why Candy is still with me?" I confessed. "Well, that's a mark of woman that is in love. That's a mark of a strong black woman. See, I have put my wife through a lot of shit over the 30 years we have been together. Cheating, fighting, jail. But no matter what, she stuck by me, made me a better man. The man you see right here, right now. Us men, we fuck up, we do things that we are not supposed to do. It's in our nature. But, when you find that right woman, hold on to her. No matter what you do, don't give up the good ones. The truly genuine woman. Because you might not find another one" Mr. Jones said to us. That's why I loved Mr. Jones. He is the father figure I have missed since my father passed. He always made us think about things, even hardheaded ass Toni.

It was about 5 o' clock in the evening when the sun started to set. Today was a good day. Everyone helped clean up; even Tasha did what she could. "Sammy, did you have a good time with your friends?" Candy asked me. "Yes I did. I am truly blessed to have a woman like you and good friends" I said to her before giving her a kiss on the lips. "Hey, cut that shit out cuz. All of us don't have anyone to go home to" Toni said to me before picking up a piece of trash. "You have momma, with her fine ass," I said to him in a joking manner. "Watch out now cuz" Toni replied pointing his index finger in my direction. "Yeah, your mom is finer than a mug" Ced added. "Y'all going to lay off my momma" Toni said raising his voice. "Aw, don't get mad Toni" Tasha said to Toni giving him a kiss on his cheek. "Watch out girl, before you have another one in there" Toni said to her before backing away. Everyone laughed except Candy and me. "Well dawg, it was good to hang out again. I'll holla later" Ced said to me. "Yeah Sammy, you know how to have a good time, with your big head" Tammy said to me. "Which one?" I replied quickly. Tammy hit me on the back of my head, gave Candy a hug and headed towards Ced's car. Mr. And Mrs. Jones gave hugs to everyone and then followed Tammy. J.R. kicked me in the leg and then ran to catch up with his mother and father. "Say Ced, you see my car? Now what's up homie?" Toni said to Ced. "Yeah, your shit is straight, I can't hate you for that, you just be careful riding around, especially where you live" Ced said to Toni giving him some dap and a hug. "You know they know me up in the hood. Ain't no one fucking with T-Roc in that bitch, but I will homie" Toni replied. Tametra and her man rolled out next. He was pretty cool, he didn't say much, hell, he didn't even tell us his name. "Hey Toni, can you give me a ride home? Candy is going to Sammy's and I don't want her to have to drive back and forth" Tasha said to Toni. Toni looked at me. "Yeah, I can give you a ride home" Toni replied. Toni grabbed her purse bag and they headed towards his car. "Alright then homie, I'll holler later. Bye Candy" Toni yelled walking behind Tasha. "Bye y'all" Tasha yelled. "Bye" Candy and I yelled at the same time. "Isn't that a funny look? Tasha and Toni? Hum" Candy said. "Maybe it was written for everything to happen like this" I replied. "Yeah, the lord does work in mysterious ways. Come on boy, I'll follow you" Candy replied to me. We grabbed the last of our things and headed to our cars.

When we got back to my house we put up all of the leftover food we had. "Man, it has been a long day, but good day" I said to Candy before sitting down on my couch. "Yeah baby and the meat you cook was so good" Candy said to me standing behind the couch, rubbing my shoulders. "Thank you baby. Damn girl, that feels good. You are about to put me to sleep" I confessed to her.

"Go ahead. Go ahead and relax, you have been on your feet since early this morning" Candy said with a soothing voice. "Yeah, but let me take out the trash first" I told her before standing up and heading for the kitchen. I grabbed the bag off the kitchen floor and headed out the front door.

The dumpster was located right across the parking lot from my apartment. When I stepped out the apartment, I looked up the street and when I did, I saw that same black truck. I watched the truck while I walked to the dumpster. I threw the trash in the dumpers and returned to the apartment. When I got to the door, the truck slowly drove off. When I stepped in the apartment, all the lights were off. "Candy" I called. "I'm upstairs" she called down to me. "Alright, I'll be up in a minute" I replied to her. I closed and locked the door. Took off my shoes and made sure all the other doors and windows were locked also. "I don't know what's up with those cats but they better leave me the hell alone" I thought to myself.

After I locked everything up, I went to the refrigerator, grabbed a wine cooler for Candy and a beer for me. I walked up stairs and when I got to the bedroom I almost dropped my beer. Candy was laid on her side on the bed in a sexy nurse outfit with no panties on. "What's all this?" I asked her. "Well, nurse Candy noticed that you are a little tired and might be in need of some medical assistance" she replied to me in a sexy voice. "Yeah, I am in need of some T.L.C" I replied to her walking towards the bed. Candy laid on her back, and spread her legs and said "Well, come and get it. Come and get your medicine". "I sure will" I replied. I sat the drinks down on the dresser on side of the bed and got down on my knees in between her legs. "Is this the feel good medicine I'm supposed to take? I asked her. "Yes, and make sure you get it all, or you won't get any dessert" she replied before pulling my head towards her pussy. I could feel the warmth from her on my face.

The pussy was already wet from anticipation of the following actions. I grabbed her by her thighs and pulled her towards me with one hard jerk. I opened my mouth wide, covering her whole pussy while slowly licking the outside walls with my tongue. The all of the sudden the phone began to ring. Candy looked at the caller id. "Sammy, its Toni." she told me. I lifted my head up "well he can call back" I replied. "Yeah, but he had Tasha with him, what if something is wrong?" Candy said while handing me the phone. "Alright. Hello" I said into the phone. "What you doing cuz?" Toni asked. "I was about to get into something nice. What's going on?" I asked. "Nothing man. Just came from Tasha's crib" he replied. "Yeah? How was that?" I asked him. "Cuz, we got to the crib and started talking. All this time I thought that she was some trick ass bitch. She really has a good head on her shoulders" Toni told me. "A good head huh?" I said back to him. "Knaw, not like that cuz. Me and her are the same in many ways. We really are. She is cool. It got me thinking" Toni said to me. "What got you thinking?" I asked him. "Well when I was driving home, the words that Mr. Jones was telling us kept ringing in my head. I need to find me a good woman. I know that I may not be in the right state of mind but I think she maybe that woman for me" Toni confessed. "Tasha, the woman for you" I asked Toni. When I said that, Candy sat up in the bed. "Like, I don't know, if the baby turns out to be mines, I wouldn't be mad. Not everyone in the world get together in the perfect situation like you and Candy. It was like faith that you found each other. I think this is faith that me and her found each other. I know the way we found each other was fucked up, but I think it had to happen this way" Toni said. "Well, you may be right. But I never heard you like this before" I confessed to Toni. "I know cuz, it's funny how things go. I don't know cuz, the feeling just came over me and if it is mines cuz, that baby won't go through the shit I went through. I'm going to be there for my baby cuz, that's on the set. But I don't want to take up your time, just wanted to talk to someone" Toni said. "Dawg, you're never taking up my time when you need someone to talk to. I will always be here for you playa. I love you dawg. You want to come by?" I asked Toni. "Knaw, you enjoy Candy's company. I need to think about some stuff. Stay up cuz" Toni replied before hanging up the phone.

I hung up the phone and sat on the floor. "Baby, what was all that about?" Candy asked me. "Toni might want to be with Tasha. Apparently they talked and really got a chance to see eye to eye on the way home. He said they chopped it up really good at her house and he wants to be the father that he never had" I replied to her. "Well what if the child isn't his? What if it's yours? Or neither?" Candy questioned. "I don't know baby. But I'm just glad that he is thinking about someone else other than himself. Toni might finally be growing up" I said to her. "Well I just hope he isn't opening himself up at the wrong time. If things don't turn out the way he wants, he may be hurt in the long run" Candy told me before sliding off the bed and hugging me. I know baby, this whole situation could be bad for all of us.

CHAPTER TEN
A glorious day turns crazy

Today was the big day. Ced and Tammy are getting married today. This morning was very busy and crazy. First of all, Tammy was all in disarray. The caterer was late, her cousins were nowhere to be found, and the cake had not showed up yet. Mrs. Jones tried her best to keep Tammy from pulling her hair out. Me and Toni arrived early so we could help out in any way that we could, but at the moment there wasn't much for us to do so we just sat and watched in amazement. "I can't believe that Ced is getting married" I thought to myself. As that thought flowed through my head I saw that Tammy's bride maids had begun to arrive. The girl's dresses were a light violet color. I'm sure glad that we were going to wear black tuxes because that color was not appealing to wear for a man.

The wedding started in about another hour and things are just now starting to come together. The cake finally showed up, Ced and the other grooms men arrived, and the guest were starting to flow in. I figured it was time for me to get myself together. I asked Mr. Jones if I could use his son's room to get dressed and he agreed. I took my tux and shoes up to J.R's room. While I was getting dressed I heard my phone ring in my pocket, it was Candy. "Hello." I answered. "Hey baby, where are you?" she asked me. "Up in Tammy's brother room getting dress, what's up?" I asked her. "I just showed up and I was wondering where you was" she replied. "Yeah, I'm almost done. I'll be done in a second" I told her before hanging up.

When I finally got done getting dressed I went back down stairs. Everything was in order and ready. I met Ced in Tammy's father's study. "Well, are you ready?" I asked him. "More than you know. Last night at the bachelor party I had so many things running through my head. I didn't even notice what was going on. I heard the music, saw the girls dancing, but nothing was registering in my brain" Ced confessed to me. "I saw that. When the girl was giving you that lap dance, your face looked very uninterested. That's why I called Paul to take your spot, and that cat really enjoyed all that ass in his face" I said to him with a laugh. "Yeah, Uncle Paul is like 100 years old. I thought he was going to have a heart attack" Ced replied with a big smile on his face. "Come on dawg, let's get out here so you can get your beautiful bride" I told him before putting my arm around his shoulder leading him out to the back yard.

Mrs. Jones did a great job decorating the back yard into the perfect place to be wedded. Ced's family sat on the right and Tammy's was on the left. I was very surprised to see how many of Ced's family that showed up. It was a long drive up from the country, but when you have a close, loving family I guess there is no distance that you won't travel to support them in whatever they do. I stood there beside Ced with the ring in my palm thinking about the day that Candy and I would get married. I want it to be a special occasion just like this one. This moment is one that I will remember forever. I scanned the crowd and I see Candy smiling at me. She must have been thinking the same thing that I had been thinking. Candy was sitting next to Tasha, Toni was sitting next to her and they were holding hands. "Wow, I wouldn't have expected that" I said to myself.

All of a sudden the "here comes the bride" music started to play. Everyone stood up and Ced took a deep breath. I put my hand on his shoulder to let him know that I was here. Tammy walked out of the house arm and arm with Mr. Jones. She was so beautiful in her wedding dress. It was an all-white, off the shoulder dress with a Vail and long train that trailed behind her. They walked slowly until they stood in front of Ced and the Preacher. "Who gives this woman?" the Preacher spoke. "I do." replied Mr. Jones before handing Tammy's hand to Ced. Ced nodded to Mr. Jones then Mr. Jones went and sat down next to Mrs. Jones in the front row.

Ced and Tammy stood hand in hand facing each other smiling as the Preacher read the vowels. "I do" spoke Tammy when the Preacher asked if she would take Ced as her lawful husband. Then Ced spoke "I do" when it was his turn to reply to the same question posed to him. I gave Ced the ring when it was time and Tammy's face lit up brighter than a Christmas tree the night before Christmas. Then the Preacher spoke "Is there anyone that objects to this union, speak now or forever hold your peace." I saw one hand go up in the crowd and I thought "oh hell knaw." It was an older woman stood up and said "did you say if you can't see go ahead and speak?" Everyone laughed and the younger lady sitting next to her whispered something in her ear. The older lady started to smile and sat down. "Aunt Mayra" Ced said to Tammy softly. After the laugher sided the Preacher spoke "Now if there isn't anything left, I now pronounce you husband and wife. You may kiss the bride" Ced took Tammy in his arms and they kissed each other softly. Everyone clapped, then Ced and Tammy walked down the aisle into the house then everyone else followed.

At the reception there was a table at the front of the room for the people that participated in the wedding. Everyone was eating and drinking having a good time when Ced leaned over to me and said "Don't you think it's time for the best man to give his speech?" "Um, not really, but I guess there is no time like the present" I said to him before standing up and tapping my glass to get everyone's attention. "I want to take this time to thank each and every one of you for making this an unforgettable experience for Tammy and Ced. It takes a lot to know what you have and be able to hold onto it. Ced found him a great woman and has always did whatever Tammy said to keep her happy. That takes a strong man, because if you know Tammy like I do, you know that she can be very demanding" I said with a laugh. Everyone in the crowd laughed also. Tammy waived her fist at me with a smirk on her face. I continue "When a man finds a woman it's a great thing, and if a woman finds a good man it's an impossible thing. Ladies, finding a good man is like finding a needle in a hay stack, then, when you find it, you hope it's not rusted from all the years of neglect it has received over the years. These two give me hope about me being with the one for me. I know that I have found her, just like Ced found Tammy. I wish you two peace, love, and fulfilling life together. I love both of you very much" I held my glass in the air and everyone else followed suit. "To the bride and groom" I spoke. "To the bride and groom" everyone spoke. I took a sip of my wine and then Ced stood up and gave me a big hug. While Ced was hugging me, Tammy stood up and tapped me on the head. Every stood up and applauded.

After that the party began. The DJ was set up in the back yard and he played all the music from our childhood. All the men, women, and children danced and had a great time. We did the Soul Train line and the Electric slide. We had a great time.

The limo came to take Tammy and Ced to the airport and they climbed in. Tammy had her head outside of the sun roof of the limo and Ced had his head out the side window. Tammy threw the bouquet before the limo drove off and Tasha caught it without even trying. Candy and I laughed so hard. "Toni what's up dawg? When is the wedding dawg?" I asked him before nudging him with my elbow. "Oh hell knaw homie" Toni replied before walking towards my car. Tasha walked over to me and Candy and smiled before clutching her stomach. "What's wrong girl?" Candy asked Tasha. "I don't know girl, I feel a sharp pain in my stomach, like a hard cramp" she replied to Candy. "Sammy get the car, this girl is in labor" Mrs. Jones told me. "Ok" I replied to her then ran towards the car. "What's going on cuz?" Toni asked me. "Tasha is in labor, we have to get her to the hospital" I told him before getting into the driver's seat of my car. Toni got into the passenger side then we drove up to where Candy and Tasha were. Toni got out and helped Tasha get into the car. Candy's car was blocked in so I told Toni "drive her to the hospital and we'll be right behind you when we get Candy's car out". Toni nodded and then drove off down the block at a high speed. The couple that had blocked Candy's car moved their car and then we headed towards the hospital which wasn't too far away.

When we arrived at the emergency room we went to the desk and asked for Tasha McDonald. The nurse told us that she was too far into labor and was taken upstairs to deliver the baby. Candy and I went to the third floor and let the nurse know who we was looking for. She informed us where the waiting room was and she would inform us on her Tasha's condition as soon as she knows more. We went to the waiting room where Toni was sitting with his head in his hands. "You ok dawg?" I asked him. "Man, that shit right there is wild. We was driving and all of the sudden she started pissing all in your car cuz" he replied. "Pissing!" I said. "No baby that was her water breaking, that wasn't piss" Candy said to me. "Wow, did it stink dawg?" I asked him. "Man, I wasn't trying to smell, I was trying to get over here. Here your key, go see for yourself" Toni told me before handing me my keys. "I'm good. I can't do anything about it now" I replied to him.

We sat in the waiting room waiting on the nurse to give us an update and it seemed like forever. Candy was getting a little worried so I went to talk to the nurse. When I was walking up the hallway a doctor passed me going the opposite way. I turned to see where he was going and saw that he was heading to the waiting room. I turned and ran back to the waiting room. When I opened the door he was asking Candy how she knew Tasha. "I'm her best friend and this is her baby daddy" she said pointing to Toni. "Well she is doing ok. The delivery was kind of rough, but we made it through. You should be able to see her in an hour or so" the doctor told us. "What about the baby?" Toni asked. "The baby is doing fine. He is getting cleaned up and you will be able to see him shortly if you want" the doctor told him. "Thank you doctor" we all said at the same time, then the doctor turn and left the room.

I was glad that Tasha and the baby were doing ok but now my mind wondered about what the baby would look like. "Would the baby look like me or Toni? And if it looked like Tasha, how would we know who the father was until the paternity test came back? How would Candy react to seeing the baby?" all these questions were running through my head. Neither one of us said much until the nurse came into the waiting room. "You can go see her now. She is in room 3b" she told us. "Thank you nurse" I told her then stood up and opened the door for everybody. When we got to room 3b Candy went in first. Toni stopped and just looked at the door in silence. "What's wrong dawg?" I asked him. "Cuz, this moment is going to change our lives forever. Once we open this door, there is no turning back" Toni said to me with a tear in his eye. "Dawg even if we don't go through this door, our lives will still be changed forever. But we are here together. We are going to handle this together. Come on, let's go" I told Toni before putting my hand on his shoulder.

Toni and I walked into the room. Tasha was laying in the bed with an IV in her arm and Candy was sitting in chair right next to the bed. Tasha looked drained and tired. "How are you doing Tasha?" I asked her. "My pussy hurts, I don't think I'm going to do this again" she replied to with a tired smile. "So you telling me that it's all stretched out? Big ass baby done came through it, how am I going to compete with that shit?" Toni asked Tasha while grabbing his dick through his pants. "Fool, it don't stay like that. After six weeks it goes back to normal" Candy snapped at Toni. All I could do is laugh to myself.

Candy moved out of the chair and sat down next to me on the love seat so Toni could sit down next to Tasha. Toni grabbed her hand and sat there looking into her eye. The room was quiet then the door opened up. The nurse came in with the baby. He was in a plastic see through cart looking thing. My heart beat began to rise with nervousness. Me, Toni, and Candy all stood up and walked over to the baby. When I looked at the baby I could have pissed my pants. The baby was the spitting image of Toni. The feeling of relief rush through my body and I could see the look of relief in the face of Candy. I looked at Toni and his face was like a stone statue. He just stood there looking at the baby emotionless.

Everyone in the room stared at Toni in silence. Then out of

nowhere I tear fell from Toni's eye and down his cheek. "Toni, pick up your boy" I said to my friend. "I don't know how" he replied to me without looking up. Candy walked over to the baby and gently picked the baby up and placed him in Toni's arms. Toni sat down in the chair and just looked at the baby then said "Hey lil homie, I'm your daddy". When he said that Tasha started to cry, Candy started to cry, hell even I let a tear drop fall. I sat back in my chair and thought to myself, this is a glorious day, but crazy at the same time.

CHAPTER ELEVEN
He will always have the father you didn't

Me and Toni left the hospital with a new outlook on life. I have never seen Toni walk so proud with his head up high, shoulders back, and his chest poked out. When we got to the car in the parking lot Toni didn't get in the car, he just stood there. "What's good dawg?" I asked him. Toni replied "I'm a father homie. I'm a father". "Well dawg, I don't know how you feel I have never been a father. How does it feel?" I asked him. "I'm proud homie. I not proud of how it became to be, but I'm proud that I have a chance to be the father that I never had. But at the same time I'm scarred. Scarred that I will become the same dad that I had, shit the same dad that he had" Toni told me. Well playa, you're the one that is ultimately going to decide what type of father that you will become. Now get your ass in the car so we can go" I told him with a smile on my face. Toni smiled and got in the car.

It had been three days and Tasha was set to leave the hospital tomorrow. Candy was doing some last minute baby shopping for the baby. I was at home alone so I decided to go out for a jog. It was a nice, cool California morning. The grass was wet from the morning dew, the air was crisp and smelled clean. I stepped outside and closed the door behind me. I started to stretch my legs so I would be loose when I started to jog. When I bent down to stretch my right leg I saw Ms. Smith walking towards her apartment door. For a woman in her mid-40's, she had a body that a 25 year old woman would die for. She had nice breast, slim waist, wide hip, and a nice petite round ass.

She had a wonderful face and a pretty smile. I always wondered why she never had a man coming around. Maybe she liked it that way. "Good morning Ms. Smith". I said to her while still bent down to my right leg. "Good morning Sammy. I see you're on your way out for a run. I was just about to invite you over for something to eat" she replied to me showing me the grocery bags in her hands. "What are you offering me to eat?" I asked her with a smile on my face. "What would you like?" she asked me. I stood up and licked my lips slightly and said "Anything wrapped in a chocolate brown shirt with pink flowers on it." She looked down and started laughing. She had on a sleeveless chocolate colored tank top and a chocolate colored skirt with pink flowers on it. She also had on some black boots that covered her legs up to her knees with six inch heels. "Boy quit before I have you leaving your girl" she replied to me. She winked her right eye at me then she walked into her apartment. I smiled and thought to myself about how nice it would be to tap that old ass.

I finished stretching and I began to jog away from my apartment. I saw Ms. Smith peeping out the front window of her apartment. I stopped running, pulled the head phones out of my ears and looked. I saw her head disappear behind the curtain, but her naked leg appeared thought the curtain. I stood there staring then I saw a breast appear through the curtain next. I couldn't believe my eyes. I thought to myself "fuck it" then I looked around to see if anyone was around then proceeded toward her door. When I started walking towards the door she completely disappeared behind the curtain. I stopped and said to myself "this old bitch is playing". Just when I was about to turn and jog away, I saw her door crack open. I took one more look around and then I jogged up to her door. I took another look around then I walk into the apartment closing the door behind me.

When I turned around I saw Ms. Smith on her knees in front of me. She immediately grabbed me by the waist of my pants pulling me towards her. "She's quite strong" I thought to myself. She loosens my draw string in my shorts then pulled my shorts down exposing my penis. My penis was slightly erect and hanging down. She looked up at me, she lowered her head down and put my penis in her mouth without using her hands. Her mouth felt amazing. My penis got hard instantly and when it did she started moving her head back and forth on it. I leaned my head back and then put both my hands on my head. She was a pro at what she was doing. She was so good that within seconds I was ready to cum. "Ms. Smith, I'm about to nut" I warned her. She didn't say anything, she just kept doing what she was doing. She started to moan and her moans vibrated quite nicely on my penis until I felt the sensation of charging flood water flowing through my penis and into her mouth. She took it all while my penis was stuck all the way in her mouth, then she stuck out her tongue and with the tip of her tongue she started to lick the bottom of my penis. "Dam, she's a freak" I thought to myself.

After she swallowed all the nut I had she took my penis out of her mouth and said "I want you to fuck me in my ass". Her voice seemed a little deeper than before but I didn't think anything of it, plus my penis was still hard so I was ready to fuck. "I don't have a condom" I replied to her. Still on her knees she leaned over to the table by the door and pulled out a condom out of the draw. She gave the condom and I immediately unwrapped it and put it on. She stood up and led me to the living room. To my surprise she still had the skirt on but her top and boots were off. "I don't smell any breakfast" I said to her with a laugh. "If you do like you're supposed to do, something will be cooking in a second" she replied to me.

She walked me to the back of the couch and she leaned over with her elbows resting on the top of the couch. She hiked up her skirt and pulled her panties to the side. She put some lube on her ass hole and before I could grab my penis, she grabbed it and slowly slid it into her ass. Her ass was so tight at first then all of a sudden it was loose. I grabbed a handful off her hair and gave it a slight pull. She leaned back off the couch and with my free hand I grabbed one of her breast and began to stroke my dick in her ass slow and deep. Her breast didn't feel like any other breast that I had grabbed before. "It must be implants" I thought to myself. I had never felt implants before. To tell you the truth it turned me on. I started stroking faster and deeper in her as until I heard her say "Yeah daddy fuck this ass like it's yours". It was kind of funny because her voice had become a little deeper than before. "I must be fucking the hell out of her ass" I thought to myself. My ego went from 60 to 100 so I started stroking faster and faster. She had a deep moan that sounded like "uuuuuuhhhh, uuuuuuhhhhh" a lot different from the "aaaahhhhh, aaaaaaaahhhhhh" I was hearing before. I laughed to myself and kept stroking until I heard a knock on the door. "Keep going" she said with a deep manly type voice.

I continued until I heard another knock at the door and some keys jingling. I jumped back and let her go. I started to pull my shorts up and started looking for the back door. "Not now" she said standing up. When she turned around I looked down at the front of her skirt and there was something pointing straight out beneath her skirt. "OH HELL KNAW!" I thought to myself. I ran to the back door. She ran behind me without saying a word and opened the back door. I ran out the back door and jumped the fence that lead outside the apartment complex. I started running down the alley until I got to a dumpster and began to start throwing up beside it. After I stopped throwing up, I reached inside my shorts and took off the condom and threw it in the dumpster. When I did, I started throwing up again. The only thought going through my head was "SHE'S A MAN, SHE'S A MAN!"

After I gathered myself, I ran out of the alley and back to the side walk next to the street. I began running down the street with the feeling of disgust flowing through my body. When I got around the corner I noticed that black Escalade parked on the other side of the street. When I passed it I heard the vehicle crank up. It made a "U" turn and began slowly driving behind me. "What now" I asked myself. I started running faster and when I did the vehicle began driving faster so I began to run faster. But the faster I ran, the faster the vehicle would go. I was in a full sprint until I said to myself "fuck it" and stopped running.

When I stopped running the vehicle pulled up beside me. I turned to the car with both my hands on my head. The passenger window rolled down. It was Big Rob and his brothers. "SAMMY! Out for a little run I see" Big Rob said from the passenger seat. "Yeah, it's very relaxing, your fat ass should try it" I replied to him. "This nigga trying to be funny, laugh now punk ass bitch!" Craig said to me before lowering the passenger window behind Big Rob then sticking a 9mm gun in my face. "I'll pull this mutha fucking trigger and it will be more than you running down this street, Mutha fucka!" Craig added before Big Rob interrupted him. "Hold on lil brother, we didn't come her for that. Where your boy Toni?" Big Rob asked me. "I don't know, and frankly if I did I wouldn't tell you if I did" I replied to him. Well frankly, nigga, your boy didn't come up with my cash or stash last night and frankly I'm tired of fucking with him and his fuck ups" "Toni stopped dealing with you a while ago" I told Big Rob. "Well, I see this nigga is a liar and a thief. But I know how to handle niggas like that. And believe me, on some real shit, its going down today" Big Rob said before the car drove off down the street.

I took out my cell phone and dialed Toni's number. The phone rang and rang until his voice mail answered. "You know who gets it poppin, leave it". I hung up the phone and dialed Toni's home number. The phone rang three times then his mother answered "hello". "Yes ma'am, is Toni home?" I asked her. "Hey Sammy, yes he is at home, hold on" she replied to me. I heard her put the phone down on the counter. I heard the phone moving and then I heard Toni's voice "what up cuz?" "Toni, Big rob and his brother's just ran up on me. They said that you owe them some drugs or some money" I told him. "Cuz, don't worry about it fool, them niggas ain't going to do anything" he replied to me. "You told me that you wasn't going to slang anymore" I said to him. "Yeah cuz, I know, but with the baby I had to get some stuff ready, but now I'm done. I'll pay Big Rob tomorrow after I put in some work tonight. Everything is cool cuz." Toni assured me. "Alright dawg, I'm heading over there" I told him. Alright, but relax homie, ok?" Toni said to me before hanging up the phone. I ran back to the apartment for a quick shower, got dressed and then drove to Toni's. On my way to Toni's house I had a tight feeling in my stomach.

When I got to the stop sign up the street from Toni's house I couldn't believe my eyes. My heart sank into my chest. Flashing police and ambulance lights in front of Toni's house. I drove up quick to the house and stopped hard on the brakes. I got out of the car and ran to the yard. When I got there I saw Toni's mother crying hysterically. I walked up to her holding back my tears. "Sammy" she said to me before wrapping her arms around me. Over her shoulder I could see the paramedics loading Toni into the back of the ambulance on a stretcher. "What happened?" I asked Toni's mother. "I really don't know. I was in the kitchen and all of a sudden I heard gun shots. I ran outside to see what was going on and I saw Toni in the front yard over there" she replied to me then pointing at her blood soak shirt. She let me go and then climbed in the back of the ambulance. The police had the yard taped off with numbered cones spread all over. The neighbors were along the tape talking among themselves. I saw Toni's phone on the ground and on the screen read "Sammy". The ambulance drove off and I asked the head detective if it was ok to lock up the house before I head to the hospital. He told me that it was ok, and that they didn't need to go in the house. I went inside the house and made sure all the windows and back door was locked.

On my way out the front door I looked to the right and saw a picture of Toni when he was a baby. He looked just like the baby that Tasha just had. I grabbed the picture and took it with me as I walked out the door.

On the way to the hospital my mind was spinning. Anger, sadness, confusion all circled my head causing my mind not to focus. I don't know exactly how I was able to drive to the hospital but I made it. When I got to the emergence room I found Toni's mom sitting in the hallway. "Where's Toni?" I asked her. "He's in surgery" she replied to me without looking up. I sat down next to her and put my arm around her shoulder. She leaned on my chest and laid there silently. About 15 minutes went by when I felt my pocket start to vibrate. I took my phone out of my pocket, it was

Candy. I didn't even answer it. I just let it go to message.

About a half an hour later the doctor came walking in our direction. I tapped Toni's mom on the shoulder and then we both stood up. "Well ma'am, it was hit and miss there for a while. We had to remove one of his kidneys and a lung, but he is stable for now" the doctor said to Toni's mom. "Can we see him?" Toni's mom asked the doctor. "I'll let you know in a few" the doctor replied before turning and walking back in the direction that he came from. "Sounds pretty good" I said to Toni's mom to give her some kind of assurance. She nodded and sat back down. I walked outside and called Candy back. "Sammy, where are you?" Candy asked me. Fighting back the tears I told her "at the hospital". "I'm at the hospital too. I'm here with Tasha and the baby. Where are you?" she asked me. I paused before I answered "I'm at the ER". "What are you doing at the ER?" Candy asked me. I paused again before answering "I'm here with Toni. He's been shot". "Oh no, here I come" Candy replied. "No, stay there and don't let Tasha know anything. He's in a stable condition and I don't know how Toni's mom is going to react to a lot of people right now. I'll call and let you know what's going on but right now, keep everything normal. I don't need Tasha getting emotional at this time" I told her. "Ok baby, you take care of her. I love you" Candy told me. "I love you too" I replied to her then hung up the phone.

I walked back into the ER and sat down next to Toni's mom again. "You know Toni's baby is right upstairs, you want to go see him?" I asked her. I do, but I don't want to leave my baby just in case something happens" she replied to me. After she said that the doctor came back out. "If you would like to see him you can, but you have to be brief" the doctor said. I helped Toni's mom to her feet and we walked to the room where Toni was. He was laying in the bed with tubes in his nose and machines hooked to him. It was silent except for the heart monitoring machine. Toni's mom walked up to the side of the bed and gave him a kiss on the fore head. Toni opened his eyes slightly and looked up. A tear dropped from his eye. She hugged his head then sat down in the chair beside the bed. I walked up the bed and smiled. Toni smiled back and nodded his head. I gently grabbed his hand. "How are you feeling?" I asked him. He took a swallow and slowly said "Like I've been shot" he replied with a smile. I laughed and said "I can see that". Toni began to laugh but started to cough. I sat down in the other chair in the room so I could text Candy when there was a knock at the door. It was Candy pushing Tasha in a wheel chair and Tasha was holding the baby. "Hi" Candy said as they entered the room. "I think someone wants to see their grandmother" Tasha said before she handed the baby to Toni's mom. "Aw, he's so cute" Toni's mom said hold the baby. "Kind of like this guy used to be" I said before taking out the picture of Toni that I took from the house and showed everybody. "I'm………still……..cute cuz" Toni said slowly. Everyone laughed. "Yes you are baby" Tasha said to Toni before giving him a kiss on the cheek from the opposite side of the bed from Toni's mom.

Toni's mom stood up holding the baby, then held the baby out in front of Toni so he could see the baby. I took out my phone so I could take a picture. In the picture a tear had fallen from Toni's eye. "Aw" everyone said. Then all of a sudden the heart rate machine started beeping faster and faster. Toni's eyes rolled in the back of his head and his body started to shake. Toni's mom pulled the baby back and stood up hold the baby close to her. "Toni baby, what's wrong" she asked. The doctors and nurses rushed in and made everyone leave the room. Toni's mom was crying so hysterically that I took the baby and gave him to Candy. I pulled Toni's mom out of the room and into the hallway. As I held Toni's mom I could see Tasha holding herself while rocking back and forth in the wheel chair. All this was going on and yet I heard nothing but complete silence in my head.

As I stood next to the coffin at the cemetery I still couldn't believe that Toni was gone. "How did we get to this point? Why?" I asked myself. Toni's mom sat holding Toni's baby and Tasha was sitting next to her. Candy was by my side as always as well as all our friends and family. It was a cloudy day and was expected to storm later on that day. But no earthly storm could compare to the storm that was going on in my body, mind and soul. "Toni I make this promise to you that your son will never want for anything. He will always have that male figure in his life that you didn't. I will be the father that you wanted to be but never had a chance to be. He will be loved just as much as I loved you. I will miss you dearly my friend. You can finally rest in peace. I love you" those where the last words I spoke to my friend before they lowered him into the ground forever.

The End

About the author

Eric James Faulk has been a freelance writer, poet and served honorably in the United States Navy. He is from a small town in Texas called Kerens. A Good Man's Guide To Becoming a Successful Cheater, Thriller at Rush Creek and She used to be my girl are titles already published by this author. Be on the lookout for his next exciting titles coming soon

www.ingramcontent.com/pod-product-compliance
Lightning Source LLC
Chambersburg PA
CBHW061753020426
42331CB00006B/1461